freedom
for
your
business

five steps to releasing yourself and
transforming your company

GILES CLEVERLEY

Re think

First published in Great Britain in 2020
by Rethink Press (www.rethinkpress.com)

Cover image © Shutterstock | Bioraven

To my family, who I strive to be better for; my parents and sister, for showing me the way and supporting the person you knew I could be.

To my children Imogen and Reece, it is my greatest pleasure to watch you grow into the people you want to be.

Contents

Introduction

A business should get easier to run the bigger it gets. This is when you can focus on building the business, not building more jobs for yourself.

Most people in business focus on the wrong things. The business is successful because they work really hard, but the aim of the business should be to become a profitable enterprise that runs just as well without them. Unfortunately, most business owners never achieve this. But we all have the same twenty-four hours in a day, so why waste them?

The main reason to get a business built and thriving without you, the owner, is that it increases your ability to choose. You decide whether you want the business to grow, raise capital, expand to extra sites, shrink (yes, this happens, often when the business has got out of control), or – the number-one goal – you decide whether to sell it (for example, when you're coming up to retirement).

Whatever it is you want, I guarantee that running and/or owning a business that operates smoothly without you is so much more fun than working yourself into the ground to keep it going. It will give you more drive, more cash in your pocket, more freedom to spend time either with loved ones, travelling or looking for new opportunities.

An important element to business is diversification. If you have multiple businesses in multiple fields, then as the world changes, they can evolve and grow without putting added pressure on you and, more importantly, your family. If one market crashes, you'll have something else to fall back on. This will allow you to sleep well at night, secure in the knowledge that even if one business struggles, you'll still have an income from the others.

Business is about understanding the customer, knowing your supplier and building your team. The only way you can build a team of great players is to have the time to develop them. You need to coach them on how to run every aspect of your business, and I mean everything. Everything in your head, every thought you have on how things should and could be done, get them into the manuals that will train your teams.

Ensure that the business grows in the right way to achieve the best possible customer experience.

This book is not about telling you to change everything. It's certainly not a golden bullet to make you a billionaire in thirty days. It offers you a practical and straightforward method to improve your businesses.

But what is improvement? What does it mean for your business? Improvement could mean increasing profit, building cash reserves, employing more people, reducing staff turnover or developing processes. The choice is dependent on you – who are you? Maybe you've just bought the business; maybe you've just started the business; maybe you've been running it for thirty years; maybe you've taken it over from a family member or friend. Your age and ideal exit age both influence what you want to improve and change in the business.

CASE STUDY – MY BUSINESS BEGINNINGS

Let's go back to 2002. I was twenty-two years old, starting out in business in a fifty-fifty partnership to run a shop. But things didn't work out and I agreed to buy out my business partner. I stood in my shop, all alone, over £80,000 in debt. I had a business that was not profitable. What was I to do?

I thought 'oh, shit!' for about thirty seconds. Then I said to myself, 'Come on, Giles, you idiot, if you don't give this 100%, you will regret it for ever.' I couldn't fail; I had to lean into it and smash it.

And I did. If I can do it, so can you. See you on the other side and we can grab a beer or lie on a hammock while our businesses continue to flourish without us.

I am not a natural academic. I am not a natural reader. At school, I never really saw the value in learning from the people around me; I was out to have fun. But when I started out in business, something changed. I was learning from people who love what they do, and love sharing the knowledge and lessons they have learned with others. And this is when learning became valuable to me.

CASE STUDY – THE ENTREPRENEURIAL ROUTE

My father always said that he loved the job he did, he just wasn't aligned with the owner of the business. With that in mind, I decided it would be better to own my business to start with. Then I could choose the way I worked and do the things I most enjoyed.

I have always believed in hard work. Work hard throughout the day and work hard in the evenings. Even when I was at university, I worked for a supermarket, a nightclub, a pub and I did market research. But I've never actually had a full-time job. I've never had the predictable wage, so I don't miss the standard amount coming in each month. After all, you can't miss what you've never had. I've always relied on myself to feed my family, and I've enjoyed every day of my working life.

The day after graduating from university, I was in a shop in a small market town, painting it ready to start my first business with a friend of mine. This was a bricks-and-mortar shop (that shows my age) selling music and games. I loved the business side of it, hustling with suppliers and getting feedback from the end user, learning everything from scratch. What did the customer want? What did we need to do for them? What did we need to sell; what could we sell? What was the shelf-life of products? The list of questions goes on and on. What a steep learning curve!

The music and games industry was great when it came to honing my ability to react to fast-moving markets, as every week there were new products being released. I soon learned that I needed to be in front of the curve when it came to purchasing by asking customers what they were looking forward to being released.

Then one big thing happened that changed everything, even though my business partner and I didn't realise it at the time. When we first opened the shop, the internet was just emerging. There was no downloading games or CDs, but this option was about to grow rapidly. It didn't take long before I realised the industry as we knew it wouldn't be there for ever.

By a stroke of luck, before we took it over, the shop had sold mobile phones, and we realised the potential growth in this industry, so we started to sell phones through the old company's network connector codes.

After a year, it became apparent that my business partner and I had different motivations, so we decided to go our separate ways and I bought the business from him. There I was, running an unfamiliar business with little or no passion for the products that I was selling. I knew music and games were not sustainable. Soon afterwards, I made my first company acquisition, buying my biggest competitor selling mobile phones in the same town. I then split the offering into two: one mobile phone shop, and one games and CD shop.

Mobile phones started to do well, and as the games sales reduced, I employed a couple of people who knew about computers. They recommended that we could start repairing computers, so that's what we did.

Essentially, if you offer a service you are reselling for someone else, you are working for a huge business that invariably prioritises its future more than that of its distributors. Over a period of about six months, all of the mobile phone networks decided they wanted to sell directly to their customers, so they cut the distributors' commissions. For us to offer similar deals, we would have lost money. Luckily, the information technology (IT) industry was suiting us more and more due to us being able to work directly with the end user.

Within a few years, we were running five stores offering IT support and larger telecoms to companies. I still own the business today, but it runs extremely well without me being involved personally, and is growing nicely.

Through businesses, property and investments, I have reached the point where I don't need to work for a living. Since my late-thirties, I have been semi-retired. Time with family is so important – I have two children and I want to be there to watch them grow up and share my life with them. Money is not the most important thing in life, but from a business perspective, it is the lifeblood.

How, then, do we get the shackles off you and your business? Easy! OK, it's not really easy, but it's definitely doable. In the pages of this book, I have broken the process down into bite-size pieces. This is the ultimate guide to get you out of your business.

How to use this book

I personally prefer to read books cover to cover and make notes. If this works for you too, the headings I normally use are:

- Must do
- People to look up
- Manuals (teams or manager)
- Posters (for me or team)
- Book ideas

Use whichever headings are relevant to you and the headspace you are currently in.

The book is based around my 5 Ws model, the Ws being:

- Why
- When
- What

- Who

- Work

Essentially, the first three Ws are personal to you. These are your reasons for wanting to take yourself out of your business. The final two Ws are about the team and the business. Hopefully, you'll be comfortable with some of the stages – feel free to move between them as you see fit – but others may need you to put in some extra hours. As with everything, nothing will change without your drive, effort and desire to make it change.

You might find it easy to read a chapter, complete some of the actions, and then move to the next. Whatever works for you, my hope is that you enjoy the book and feel by the end that it has been a good investment of your time.

Some solid advice I would give to everyone is to buy a journal and make notes as they come to you. If, when reading, you see something interesting, or you want to make sure you look up a certain person, or you think something would make a great poster, make notes to come back to it later. Carry them around and keep them for reference. You will likely want to come back to them sometime in the future.

Finally, a bit of plain speaking: this is not a book for lazy snowflakes who think the world owes them a favour. Business is hard. It takes hard work, discipline and resilience, but the rewards are well worth the climb.

PART ONE
WHY?

Why do you need freedom from your business?

1
I Need To Get Outta Here!

You need to free yourself from your business. Why?

What a great question. Why do we do things? Why do we like what we like?

I've often heard people with successful businesses that are generating good profit saying, 'No one else can do what I do.' Sorry, but if you think this, you're *wrong*. What you actually mean is, 'No one else is trained to do the task I currently do.'

This is by far the most important thing you need to establish. Why do you want to change your business structure or what you do with your time? What will you do with this extra time? Once you know why you want to generate extra time, you will become more focused. You will get to your target more quickly – fact! You might be looking at a five- to ten-year plan.

The mind strives for what it sees and believes, so you need your mind to see the 'other side' – the ultimate goal. The why. Then you can get you, your business and everything else there.

There are numerous reasons why people want to work their way out of their business or day job. You need to crystallise yours before you can start working towards it. Then you will accomplish your goals.

What's your raison d'être, your why for extracting yourself from your business? These are the main responses I hear when I ask this question:

- To sell the business
- To prepare it to be floated on the stock exchange
- To create a passive income generator (PIG)
- To become a chairperson with overall say, but not the day-to-day bottlenecks
- To retire by selling the business
- To retire by passing it on

Let's look at each one of these common whys in more detail.

Sell the business

Preparing to sell lock, stock and barrel is certainly the easiest way to remove yourself from your business. It takes the emotion away from all the operations, so you can look at your roles and gradually work yourself out of them.

When looking at selling your company, do a complete review of the business. What would it look like when it's achieved everything it's set out to achieve?

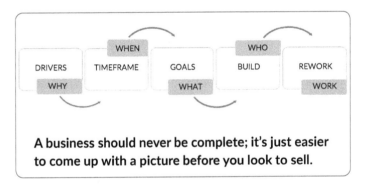

A business should never be complete; it's just easier to come up with a picture before you look to sell.

This can be a good time to get the company valued. What's it worth today? What could it be worth when it matches your image of completion? Who will be the best person/company to buy it to give you the maximum return?

Answering these questions shows the external situation of the business. For example, how is the market it's in lying? Is it growing? Will the business need to diversify in the mid- to long-term? If it has to diversify in the short-term, I'll assume you are already in the process of change.

You do not have control of this market valuation from the external perspective. For example, if your market size is £1 billion, no amount of restructuring can alter this.

You can then look at who will buy the business and focus on them. Is it an individual? Usually restaurants, for example, are purchased by individuals. How about your biggest competitors? Are they bigger than you in turnover – perhaps 3× size? If you have, say, ten locations, is your profit a direct 10× multiple? There's a lot to think about in terms of your valuation.

Once you know what the business's current market value is, you can look at what you want it to be worth, which can vary by many multiples. Many people says £10 million or £100 million, but is that really what you want to sell it for? You need to get to a valuation that is a stretch, but not a fairy tale. If the target is too big, it will seem unfeasible and will just be a random number that no one pays any attention too.

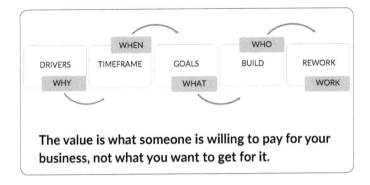

The value is what someone is willing to pay for your business, not what you want to get for it.

You need a goal figure as it focuses the mind and gives clarity. Once you have a financial goal, you then need a time goal. This can really be a game changer.

If you are aiming for an age goal – for example, you want to retire by a certain age – this can be more powerful than a financial goal. You need to know this when you implement the planning stages as you will ultimately map out how to adjust the business and, more importantly, yourself and the way you see your business. At this stage, you will look at who within the business will help you. Not everyone on the team will want to be your ally – human nature is to fear change and lean against it.

At this stage, look at the business as a whole and break it down into sections. Some call this a 360° review. Others call it how to eat an elephant (in bite-size pieces, of course).

These sections generally come under:

- Production (whether you offer a product or a service)

- Finance

- Sales

- Marketing and advertising

The roles, depending on the size of your business, may cross over or you may be able to break them down into more detail. In fact, the more detail, the better. The main thing to ensure is that you cover everything and don't neglect any department or actions (regardless of how big or small) integral to the operation of the business.

What you are aiming to do – as with everything we'll cover in this book – is arrive at your desired destination. Always remember, though, that any change is a process, not a one-off event.

This is a good time to work out the structure of the business (I will be going into more detail in Chapter 6). Look at how the business runs. Is there potential for ironing out many of the bottlenecks that may be present? Continually ask the question, 'Why do we do what we do in this department, and how can we improve it?'

Float the company on the stock exchange

She's a strong vessel. But will she float?

Floating is similar to selling the business, but is more about how it is running, how many assets it has and its overall worth to the stock market. This can create more of a work burden. You are likely to be used to having control and being able to make most of the decisions; now, you will have to give away that sole command as you will have a board of directors to answer to.

SIDE NOTE – WHAT IS WEALTH?

If you work for a company and are suddenly made redundant, how will it affect you? What if your business goes bust? Investing in property and shares is a great way of making sure you don't put all your eggs in one basket.

An example of wealth is this: if someone has outgoings of £2,000 per month and they lose their job – if they have £2,000 in the bank, they will run out of cash in one month. If the same person has investments that pay £1,000 per month, their money will last two months. If they have investments that pay £3,000 per month, they are truly wealthy and essentially financially retired.

The true measure of wealth: if your main form of income stopped tomorrow, how long would your lifestyle last until the money ran out?

The stock exchange is looking for raw data initially, so you need to place emphasis on the position of the business and its market share. It is surprising how few people have defined their marketplace, let alone analysed the numbers and the worth of the share they currently control. Also, you need to position the business to justify your place within it. Often the business owner doesn't see mass value until the float happens, which can be a long and weary road. Make sure that you want this 100% as it is usually costly upfront.

If you decide to value the business, you can usually get a value for both floating and selling. As the stock market largely looks at your business from a financial basis, you need to look at your financial positioning; so if you currently have debt, then you may have to adjust the timing. If you have loans that are due to complete in three years, then you may decide to aim to float the business after that. Or you may want to settle with a bridging loan for the interim.

This is a vast area, so I don't want to go into exact details. I would always recommend getting specialist help and advice.

Create a PIG

Everyone loves a PIG. This is where you have no/ minimal physical input into the company and it doesn't take up any of your time; you just watch the money come into your bank account.

You need to know how much passive income you require, so you know how much money the PIG needs to generate. For example, say you are moving abroad and need £10,000 per month to live, or you're starting another business that will take up all your time, but will need to be financed for the first six months at £30,000 per month. This is something you will need to plan and make allowances for.

Will the PIG in its current state give you the returns you need? Do you need to expand it first? By how much? If the goal is to double the business's profit, you first need to thrash through the numbers and make sure you have a clear thirteen- or twenty-six-week rolling cash-flow forecast, as overstretching on a new project may bring down the existing business.

There are literally hundreds of ways to create a PIG. Here are a few things to think about:

- What are you looking to expand the business to?

- Do you want to break it up?

- Is breaking it up, selling it or giving it away an option?

- How about franchising the business? This can mean a huge shift, often reducing the size of the core business.

- Could you expand the core of the business? You would need to have targets and know which areas to do this in. Will you need extra teams? I'll cover this in more detail in Chapter 6.

- Geographically, is the business national or international?

- What stage of expansion is it in? If you are currently at a single location and want to expand into multiple, this can be a huge change for everyone within the business. If you are already in multiple sites and want to expand abroad, you may want to look at the possibility of partnering with a business that already has connections and local knowledge.

You will need to look at why you may feel the need to expand. Alternatively, merging with a competitor can be a really good method of working your way out of the business while using their resources. If they have an executive team and structure, you could be at an advantage if you use them, too.

I could write another whole book on this. All I would stress here is that you must complete a lot of due diligence before you decide on this type of merger. If the companies do not align, you can spend £millions to get out of the agreements, and your business will really suffer in the meantime. Sometimes, it can break a business.

Become a chairperson

This is usually the most popular aim founders of companies have, but seldom do they write it down as a goal. It's usually in the back of their heads that it will happen one day, but failing to plan is planning to fail.

Getting the business to the point where it can truly run without you so you only make the top-level decisions is something that you should be planning for many years in advance. This is the sweet spot of owning a business, but fewer than 4% of company owners get there, and this is largely through the fear that they will no longer be needed. Watch out for Superman syndrome!

Most businesses are built up around the owner (both subconsciously and consciously, this is how the owner creates their business). As soon as something adverse happens – a machine breaks down or a client complains – the owner puts on their superhero cape and comes to the rescue. Mark my words, this is a huge red flag to any investor.

What you want to aim for is to become financially retired. When I talk about retirement, I don't mean you should move into an old people's home. Financial retirement enables you to work because you *want* to, not because you *have* to. Work becomes fun when you choose to do it.

You need to get to know your figures. The plan might be to acquire a buy-to-let property every year for ten years, so the ten-year goal is absolute financial retirement. Then consider where you would like to navigate (run) the business from. If it is abroad, you need to put the right processes and structures in place.

Financial retirement

Your aim is financial retirement. Whether you show up to work or not, you still have an income that pays all your bills and maintains the lifestyle you are accustomed to.

Generally, all people get to a stage in their lives when they feel enough is enough and they would like to stop working. In the traditional sense of retirement, this is age sixty-five-ish, depending on what country you are living in.

In my experience, most company owners and directors retire when they feel the time has come or their significant other makes the decision for them. Retirement can be at any age, whether it's thirty or ninety. Possibly spending more time on charitable works is an incentive to retire. Or retirement can happen as a natural consequence of passing the business on to a son or daughter. This can be a powerful driver. Getting the stake in the ground, ie deciding on a specific date for your retirement, is a good start.

Everyone's why is different, and your why is your own. Your raison d'être is inside you, but you may not have explored your why. In fact, most people never really explore their why.

A person's why often aligns with that of someone else, a spouse or child's usually. And it can change. Bill Gates, founder of Microsoft, whose why was once to see a personal computer in every home, now fully focuses on the Bill and Melinda Gates Foundation to improve the quality of life for everyone. I'm not saying yours should be that big, but I'm sure you get the picture.

CASE STUDY – IT'S MAGIC!

Let's perform some magic. Go back to when you were a child and could dream and believe. Go on, try it. Close your eyes, I promise I won't tell anyone (but don't forget to keep your place in the book).

I would like to share a story with you that I feel sums up the search for your why, and the magic that can happen when you retrain yourself to think as a child. A school invited all its pupils and their parents in for a gathering. When everyone was assembled, the headteacher asked all the parents to raise their hands if they could sing. Only three parents out of two hundred raised their hands. Then the head asked the same question of the children. Straight away, all the kids raised their hands.

Somewhere along the line, we lose our beliefs. Reconnect with your inner child and find your why.

Now we have started to build a picture of what your future will look like, let's examine the processes to get you there. Remember this is to get you to where you want to be, no one else.

Key takeaways

There are any number of reasons why you may want to extract yourself from your business, six of which we have looked at in this chapter:

- To sell the business

- To prepare it to be floated on the stock exchange

- To create a passive income generator (PIG)

- To become a chairperson with overall say, but not the day-to-day bottlenecks

- To retire by selling the business or passing it on

Which is yours? And how will you ensure the business will continue to grow and thrive without you?

It is essential to find your why before you strive for your goal. Let go of your serious adult side and allow your imagination to soar like a child's. That's where you will find your all-important why.

2
Drive

Laziness is for the weak. Will you choose to be weak or strong?

Drive makes the difference for all businesses, large or small. How much drive has the team got? The board? The owner and/or managing director? Drive is what many individuals will follow and respect more than anything else in a person. Most of us want to be known as someone who gets things done, but the core of that is the drive to achieve.

You have probably heard of people who have breakdowns in one form or another after losing their drive. There are two main ways of getting and keeping drive, and to be the most you can be, you need a combination of them both. The first is the voice in your head that gets you up in the morning and feeling pumped. The other is your drive, which splits into:

- Internal – the people around you who influence you, such as loved ones, friends, family, business partner etc

- External – business coaches, consultants, mentors etc

The main factor of differentiation is that group one will have a subconscious effect, both positive and negative. Group two offers drive directly, a guide to follow. And we all need to have our reaching point, our aiming point. What is yours? What do you look towards and aspire to?

How do you first break into drive? A lot of this is mindset: you need to get into the right frame of mind to drive yourself and others forward. When you start, others will follow. People are attracted to those who are going places. They will come along for the ride, so hold on tight. It will be bumpy, difficult, frustrating but, most of all, it will be worth it.

For many of us (myself included), connecting within ourselves is harder to do than connecting with random strangers. Put me in a room full of people I don't know and I'm happy and confident. It's easier to pretend with others – 'How are you?' 'I'm fine, thank you. And you?' 'I'm fine too.' But you can't pretend with yourself, so it really is a question of mind over matter. Being authentic and real requires you to own your beliefs, fears, emotions, limitations and vulnerabilities.

In terms of handing the business over to someone else, our biggest fear can be: 'No one will run and drive the business as well as me'. Firstly, let's get rid of this head trash. There will never be a perfect person to run any business – fact. We need to nurture people, giving them a sense of meaning and purpose so they want to drive the business forward. Remember, people must want to drive things for themselves.

Equally, no one wants to work at a crappy company. Everyone wants to be on a winning team. You can offer people loads of cash, but eventually this will not help. You need to retain talent on a deeper level, which can take many years.

Pedal to the metal

In the context of this chapter, I want you to rely on self-drive, as you need the drive within yourself to complete the biggest mind-shift journey you have ever taken. Let's start at ground zero. How did you get to where you are today? Some will be good at answering this, but for others, it will be a whole new world.

I don't expect you to sit in the lotus, or even half lotus, position and tap your thumb and forefinger together, although if you find it helps, then feel free. I'm talking about positive reinforcement throughout the day to give you a lift and drive you to aim for your goals (we will be discussing goals in Chapter 5). And we need to get you doing this automatically so it doesn't disrupt your day.

SIDE NOTE – MINDSET

Just a quick note on mindset. I'm not talking about suddenly turning into Gandhi, but you do need to think about the person you want to become before you become that person for real.

A good example of people not being ready for something is when those who have always struggled financially win the lottery. They are unprepared for the sudden financial freedom, so they don't know how to deal with it, and consequently it makes their lives worse and less fulfilled than they were before. The initial happiness of giving up work, buying a big house and flash cars, and taking lavish holidays soon wears off, and what is next for them?

Usually their life runs out of purpose. Their old life has gone as their friends are still moaning about money and the boss and Monday morning, so they can find themselves drifting and alienated. This is why over 70% of lottery winners end up broke.

You need to make sure you don't go the same way. Constantly upgrade and change your meaning and purpose.

In the 1940s, Abraham Maslow introduced the idea of a Hierarchy of Needs, which has five main levels:

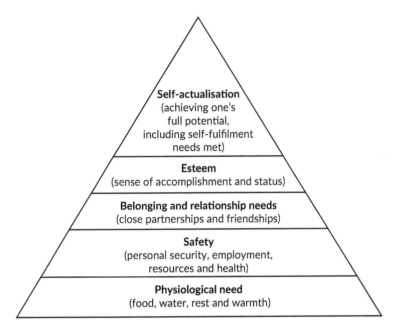

- The basic level is the need for food and shelter

- The stages in-between cover safety, belonging and esteem

- The ultimate stage is legacy

We can see the legacy stage with Bill and Melinda Gates. Now they have amassed huge wealth, their legacy is to help the world's poor through their foundation. When Bill first started out developing Microsoft, do you think he was aiming to conquer world famine and poverty? No, he upgraded his goals and aspirations as he and his wealth grew.

Affirmations

Affirmations can be powerful – give them a try. You need to come up with ten things that you really want to be in the next one to five years. For example, you might say 'I own a five-bedroom house with a swimming pool worth £2 million in March 20XX' or 'I have a golf handicap of four in September 20XX'. It can be whatever you dream about, but the key is to make it specific and emotional.

'I am' statements are essentially personal to you, but it's key to have a mixture of business and personal affirmations. Remember, your business is only there to allow you to achieve your personal goals, so if having five PIGs is your aim, make sure this is where your mindset is.

Always express your affirmations in the present tense, as if you have already achieved them. And use pictures to describe your statements. Personally, I am a visual person, so pictures really bring my affirmations to life. Possibly a place, a song or a scent will evoke feelings and emotions in you.

The mind is so powerful – it will take you wherever it is focused. Use this as your roadmap to where you want your life to go.

I would suggest revisiting your affirmations at least every six months, and make sure you're reminded of them regularly:

- Have your number-one goal stuck to the bathroom mirror, so you see it every morning

- Record your 'I am' statements and listen to them when you are walking the dog or going for a run

- Have them as your screensaver so you see them every day (set the screensaver for one minute, not the standard five minutes)

- Print them on a business card that lives in your wallet so you can read them every day or week

- Create a slide show of short, snappy statements using PowerPoint, then download it onto a digital photo frame for your desk with your affirmations constantly rotating

- Voice record them onto your phone and listen to them on a cycle when you're driving

- Stick them to the palm rest on your laptop or MacBook

- Put notes in your shoes

- Tape them to your car's steering wheel or sun visor

- Add as notes to your e-readers

The list is endless.

Affirmations can be quite hard to get into. You might need to clear your head trash and just go for it, but eventually you will feel the change happening.

Where there is focus, there is growth

I know of people who put their three- to five-year goals on a poster, and then needed to upgrade it after eighteen months. You are likely to be surprised how fast you can reach your goals when you really focus on them.

CASE STUDY – DIFFERING MINDSETS

I was at an event hosted by Brad Sugars (the founder of ActionCOACH) where he described living in both Australia and the United States. In the United States, he pulled up to a crossing and a guy gave him a big thumbs-up and shouted, 'Awesome car, well done.' Same situation happened in Australia and the guy shouted, 'Look at that tosser!'

The mindsets of people vary all over the globe. Most people driving expensive cars have worked hard for them; fewer than 5% are given these things or born into wealthy families.

Start appreciating the things and people around you and help them grow. Never set out to bring people down; focus on what you can achieve. Mind your own s**t and let other people worry about theirs.

An essential part of the focus mindset is to associate with likeminded people – those who get your aspirations, and will support you rather than hold you back. A smoker will never want you to give up smoking; it is always the ex-smoker or non-smoker who will encourage you. The alcoholic will always want you to have one more drink, but is the extra drink really for you or for them? I am not telling you to ditch all your friends, but you may possibly need to add to your social circle.

Business networking can be a great way of doing this, which is why golf and country clubs are good places to make new business and social contacts. Gyms, masonic lodges, churches, round tables, rotary clubs – the list of places for you to seek out likeminded people is endless.

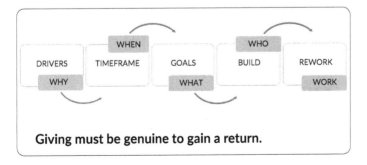

Giving must be genuine to gain a return.

If you are unsure about meeting and sharing ideas with different people, a business coach or consultant can be a great connector. I am a huge advocate of business coaching as it can be a good sounding board for your ideas and great for giving you a different perspective on things. At least try a business coach of some kind.

Depending what you are looking to achieve, consider having an accountability buddy, whether it is a business coach who you pay, or someone you like and trust from a networking event. It doesn't have to be at a business level; it could be someone you play sports with. To help you get rid of some head trash, parents or siblings can work well, as they will always want the best for you. That said, I would recommend finding someone who is unbiased and candid. There are enough people who will blow smoke at you; go for the truth when it comes to a mentor or coach.

You could look at creating a group online. LinkedIn, for example, can be a really good way of communicating to the outside world, and there will always be people willing to listen and give their feedback, too. Warning – for all the positives, there will generally be a negative. Don't worry. It is what it is, so f**k 'em.

CASE STUDY - NOT SO DUMB

A great story of relentless drive is that of the actor, Jim Carrey. In 1985, he wrote himself a cheque for $10 million, dated for Thanksgiving (that falls in November) 1995. The cheque was for 'acting services rendered'. In November 1995, he got the contract and $10 million for his part in the movie *Dumb and Dumber*.

However you find your drive, I suggest you try something. Anything. You really do have nothing to lose.

Drive of the team

Leadership requires two critical components:

- Belief from followers
- Self-belief

It can be a major advantage if you can get the team behind you, but sometimes you may feel that they don't have drive and you need to position them better. No one wants to work for a dead-end company; they will follow inspired leaders and businesses that are going places.

It is hard to appeal to all people, but if your team members at least like and trust you, you're halfway there. If you create a buzz around your people and business, they will literally take the bull by the horns and drive the business forward. But you must get the people around you fired up or you will never get the business to any of the stages we spoke about in Chapter 1.

Remember, people will follow any leader, but they will give blood, sweat and tears for a visionary leader who expresses more than someone who only has management acumen. Be the person who inspires others to be all they can be. This can take years of self-development, but it will be worth it.

Your attitude must inspire others. If you are a miserable sod who slumps about with your head down, how can you expect others to follow you and be driven by you? Ask yourself, 'Would I be inspired by me?'

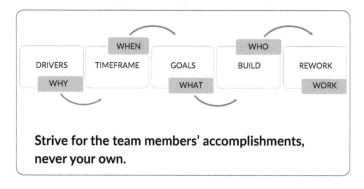

Strive for the team members' accomplishments, never your own.

Key takeaways

Drive can come from two sources: inside yourself and those around you. The essential thing is creating and maintaining the right mindset to drive forward towards your goals. This mindset, and the resultant drive, can come naturally from:

- Positive reinforcement

- Affirmations

- Focus on your goal

- Your team – be inspirational and your people will sweat blood for you

Now you have a clearer idea of what you really want and a roadmap to get you there, let's look at that most valuable of commodities: time.

PART TWO
WHEN

Aim, plan, go!

3
Your Time

Time is the ultimate resource that no one can get back, but many seem to be happy to either waste it or give it away for free. Stop it, right now. Know the value of your time. It's imperative.

We all have 86,400 seconds in a day, that's 31,536,000 seconds in a year, so we will be lucky to live 2,522,880,000 seconds (eighty years). The key question is, what will you do with these seconds you have been given? When you focus on what you do best, on what brings you the most satisfaction, there is plenty of time for everything.

This is the part I want you to really sit back and think about. You only have one life, one chance, and if you are naturally lazy or you spend all your time doing things you do not enjoy, you need to change this.

Being in flow

When you are doing things you enjoy, you are 'in flow'. Essentially, things seem easy to do. You want to complete them to the best of your ability and, more importantly, you enjoy doing them.

Most people jump out of bed on the weekend as they are looking forward to doing something they enjoy, but Monday to Friday, they are miserable and hit the snooze button ten times. You need to be jumping out of bed, raring to go every day – not only at weekends.

How can you get your work week in flow? How do you get to wanting to jump out of bed every day, because you cannot wait to get stuck into your work?

First and foremost, you need to start with the big question: 'What do I actually spend my time doing?' You must start here before you can move on to the fun bit of getting your time back.

Create two different time diaries: a guestimate diary and a real-time diary. Your guestimate diary covers the year you've just passed. Look roughly at how you think you spent your time over the past year. Include everything that stands out and has been memorable.

I always find that doing this freehand using a piece of A3 paper and different colours is good. Use the different colours for business or personal activities/ projects. Then look at what aspects were good and bad – I use red pen for bad, green for good.

CASE STUDY – PAINTING THE HOUSE

If you spent two weeks painting the house, let's say that potentially cost you £5,000 in unbilled work time, so you need to work this through as you could probably have paid a painter £1,000.

You can go two ways: either look at generating £4,000 extra, or work for a week (generating £2,500), pay the painter and have a week on a yacht with the other £1,500. This is still the block of two weeks of work time, but the trick is to look at how you could spend the time in the best way for you. What will you most enjoy doing, for you?

When you have created your guestimate diary, you need to look at what you *chose* to do and what you were *made* to do. This element is huge. Remember, your overall goal is to only do things you want to do. What is the point otherwise?

Many things you might not like, but you have to do them, such as paying bills. If you put a system in place and get someone else to check them, you no longer need to get annoyed by the cost of electricity or telephone calls. You are likely to be amazed at how much more relaxed you will feel without stressing about the many things you ultimately cannot control.

You can use your guestimate diary as a benchmarking tool for the year ahead. Keep coming back to it for reference.

Then you move on to keeping a real-time (what's happening today) diary. This is where you will spend two to four weeks writing down everything you do in a day. Yes, that's right, record every single thing you do.

There will be many things you may want to keep. For example, walking the dog is good for exercise and thinking time, but standing watching the kettle boil may not be such a wise investment of your time. Perhaps an automatic water boiling machine would be a good idea.

You need to know everything, and this includes all the 'time bandits': people who ask you stupid questions or get you to deal with a customer query when they should have dealt with it themselves. The more detail you add to your real-time diary, the faster the results will come through.

I once completed a time study with my team members. On the surface, it looked like all they did was answer the phone and complete quotations, but we discovered that they were using three to four hours per day on emails. As a result, we were able to implement five good rules for emails to save us at least 50% of that time.

Once you have a detailed overview of how your day gets used, you look at how you can slide the scale. Firstly, you need to highlight the things you enjoy (this can take a while, but is truly worth it). Then you start offloading the rest.

SIDE NOTE - YOU ARE YOUR BIGGEST BOTTLENECK

Most managers think they are helping everyone when they intervene in the day-to-day running of the business. But often they are so overloaded, they are more of a hindrance.

Do you delegate to others? If so, do you need to recruit (we'll be covering this in Chapter 8) or have you already got people you can delegate to? Should you outsource? (We will discuss outsourcing in Chapter 9.) Whatever the answers to these questions, you will need to concentrate on getting your business procedures and processes slick and making sure that your teams are fully trained to do the job better and more consistently than you currently can (this is the real wakeup call). You might need to spend years training your staff on a lot of the tasks, but first you need to break down exactly what you do, before you can delegate.

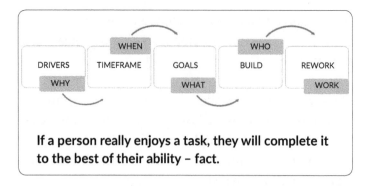

If a person really enjoys a task, they will complete it to the best of their ability – fact.

Involve your team

I have a great tip to share with you: *ask the team*. It is important that you do not bring a monetary element into it at this stage. Just as you ask yourself which tasks you enjoy doing, you need to ask the same question of your teams. You don't want to delegate a task to someone who doesn't want to do it, won't enjoy doing it and will do a poor job of it.

CASE STUDY – PROFILING

Here is a great case when profiling came into play (we'll cover profiling in more detail in Chapter 9). Many years ago, I profiled four key members of my team, initially to understand how each one fitted into the team and why they did the things they did.

Ultimately, I wanted a complete redo of the employee manual. I ended up giving the job to the last person I would have chosen to complete the task, but his profile highlighted him as detail orientated and creative. He ended up doing an excellent job, far better than I could have done and, more importantly, he really enjoyed it.

When you have your monthly routine and non-routine tasks to hand, grade them. Keep it nice and simple:

- 1–10 on how easy the task would be to delegate to someone else

- 1–5 on how much you like doing the task

- 1–5 on how urgent it is

Choose the least important, least fun things to delegate first. Remember, this is not abdicating the role; it's enabling others who will enjoy the task. There really is nothing more satisfying than seeing the things you dislike doing getting delegated and realising your teams are completing them perfectly well without you. In fact, as long as the process and procedure is solid, they're likely to do it better than you.

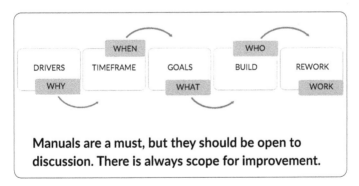

Manuals are a must, but they should be open to discussion. There is always scope for improvement.

Make sure you discuss all procedure manuals with your teams, making clear that they are merely a guide towards the best way to complete a task. They can always be tweaked and altered.

Once you have your delegation list, it can be printed and stuck on your wall. You can then use a wall planner to keep everyone accountable. Remember, *everyone* must be on board with this. And you have to make sure everyone is allowed to fail. It is OK for anyone to fail, as long as they don't do it through stupidity or laziness, and they learn from it. Thomas Edison failed to invent the lightbulb over 1,000 times – or did he find 1,000 ways not to make a lightbulb? But if someone is doing a task to the best of their ability and they still fail, you need to assess the way your training and systems are set up.

SIDE NOTE – LET IT GO!

If you are struggling to delegate, to let go, I suggest you play this game. You need to do this with either your management team or a family member, just as long as the people you choose are willing to be honest with you.

Get your list of things you do. For every task, stand up (it's important you do it standing as it activates the receptors to get your mind open) and ask the person with you, 'Why did I do this and not someone else?' or 'Why do I do it rather than someone else?' Another way of looking at the different tasks is to ask, 'What would happen if I didn't do it?'

Bringing this out in the open makes you and everyone else accountable. Now you can really put your list into bite-size chunks that can gradually be delegated away from you.

How to delegate

Remember how delegation works. Your main priority is to take the responsibility of getting the task completed to a high standard away from yourself. The person you initially delegate the completion of the task to may decide to delegate it to another person, and that is fine. Support them in this, unless they are abdicating their responsibility.

Depending on the size of your team, once you get rolling with this process, you can complete it as you go through the layers of management. Grading tasks with a view to delegating a large proportion of them is a great tool, especially as many people don't understand how much time they're wasting on menial tasks. People rarely offer to do more tasks, but if they have 100% ownership over a task, they will want to complete it fully and properly.

At some point, you learned how to do a task, so you can 100% teach someone else. Whether it takes six months or six years, it *will* be worth it. The golden question to ask is: 'How can I help you to achieve this? What time and resources do you need?'

Remember, human nature is to aspire and evolve. Rarely will people aspire to take the route of least resistance; they take it only if they feel they can't make a difference. Your team doesn't want to work for a piss-poor company. Give them Northern Lights to follow, helping them, nurturing them and guiding them in the right direction.

Then you need to put measures in place to ensure things are happening as you expected. Benchmarks and key performance indicators (KPIs) are imperative. All too often, people rush offloading tasks, then they neither give their team members enough training nor monitor the quality standard. After a few months, they're left wondering why the team is struggling with poor quality or a high staff turnover.

There are no right or wrong measures as many companies have lots of different processes. I would suggest looking at a selection of measures, then reducing them down for daily, weekly or monthly viewing. When you feel the need, you can view the full unabbreviated figures from the business.

How fast the business is growing usually impacts on the types of measures you use and the frequency of measuring. I suggest reading *Scaling Up* by Verne Harnish[1] if you are struggling with this.

---

1   V Harnish, *Scaling Up: How a few companies make it... and why the rest don't – Rockefeller Habits 2.0* (Gazelles, 2014)

The first place to start is to break down the different departments of the business, for example finance/production/sales/delivery. You can then take each of these and break them down further. For example, if you are in manufacturing, you will need a lot of measurements in production.

You are currently the captain of the ship. For the ship to go faster, slow down and dock without you at the helm, everything you put into place has to operate without you being there. And you need to make sure whoever takes the helm after you is not put in the same situation as you are in currently.

There are two main reasons for this:

- They may get snowed under and not perform well.

- If they leave, the business will suffer, inevitably resulting in you being sucked back in.

When you have a breakdown of what you do all day and the areas you are pivotal to in the business, look at reshaping to get the business running without you.

Key takeaways

Time – we all have the same amount of seconds in a day, but once they're gone, they're gone. What tasks are you doing that are not a good investment of your precious time? What gets you out of bed, raring to go, and what causes you to hit snooze ten times each morning? It could be that those tasks you hate will be the exact things that get a team member excited and in flow.

The important things to remember when delegating are:

- Involve your team in the discussion

- Keep the discussion ongoing

- Profile your team and recruits to make sure the task fits the person and everyone works in flow

- Put the correct measures in place to make sure the business continues to run and grow as you want it to

- Use processes and manuals well to ensure those who come after you can do the job as well if not better than you

- Make sure your processes and manuals evolve with the business

- Make sure neither you nor your team are abdicating responsibility under the guise of delegating

Time is an asset. Let's now look at the amount of time you are willing and need to invest in planning to future-proof your business.

4
Planning

Set the plan, achieve the plan – simple! To reach your goal, you need to understand why you want it and by when, then plan backwards. You know your destination, so work backwards until you arrive at today.

If you do not have a timescale, your goal will probably not happen, or at best it will take longer than it should have. The mind works better when it has a truly tangible target. Take an Olympian as an example. Every time they train, it is with the goal of winning gold at the next Olympics in mind. If they just bumble along procrastinating, they will miss their window of opportunity and never achieve their true potential.

This chapter is your gold medal.

In the context of planning and timescales, let's look at my top reasons to adjust the business so it runs without you. Some of them will apply to you, some will not, so take what you need from this chapter. You need a minimum of six months, but the optimum timescale for this adjustment is two to three years. If you do not have this long, then you will need to adjust your timescales accordingly.

Succession planning

This is the main reason people are prompted to work on the structure of the business. They are looking to retire and do not want their business to crumble as soon as they leave. Most people will empathise with you wanting to retire and/or pass on the business, so this is the nicest environment in which to make changes.

I recommend reading *Winning* by Jack Welch.[2] He talks about how the number-one job of a leader is to build a succession plan. This keeps the business stable and means you don't have to headhunt for the position and pay your successor a lot of money.

Look at the timescales. Hopefully you have two to three years before you want to exit the business. You then need to look at the personnel you'll require to allow you a smooth and celebrated exit.

---

2   J Welch, *Winning* (Harper, 2005)

First of all, look internally. Who can do what you are doing? If you are retiring and your son or daughter is taking over, you need to look at their capabilities today. Scale their training so they will be able to do everything you currently do, or potentially reshape the business so they operate from a high level and delegate some tasks that you currently do to others within the organisation. Either way, you need to do this well before you look at exiting the business.

This may be a good time to make sure your successor wants the business. You may have to sell the idea to your children, so it's worthwhile discussing this upfront. There is nothing worse than seeing a successful, solid business being run into the ground by undeserving offspring wasting all the hard work of their predecessors.

Remember, you don't just want to take the work from one person and dump on to another; you need the business running well structurally, so multiple people must be able to do fully systemised tasks backed up by written and video manuals. Then when people are on holiday, go sick long-term or leave the business, it won't affect the day-to-day operations.

If the business has solid systems and procedures in place, you will be able to recruit great people with great attitudes to run those systems. This is the foundation for a stable culture within the organisation. If you need to recruit, come up with the ideal candidate by profiling the type of person you need. (We'll go into more detail in Chapter 9 about profiling people.)

Think of the types of businesses that inspire you, or that you want your business to emulate, then watch YouTube clips of the CEO and other important figures. You can usually draw on their profiles.

Succession planning is also a time to look at external companies for help. A good headhunter or recruitment company is worth their weight in gold, but a bad one can be a real drain on time and resources, and cause huge frustration. I would always recommend interviewing a few different ones to see how well they 'get' you and your business.

Remember, succession planning should be detailed in your will, so if you were to die suddenly, it would continue. Key person insurance can be a worthwhile investment to look into, too. Even if you have no intention of exiting your business, having a clear plan and starting the process can be helpful. I would recommend all company owners have this type of plan in place. At least outline the main tasks you do to keep the business running in your absence.

A lot of good businesses go under due to the executives not knowing clearly what anyone else does daily. Do you have clear company goals, values and rules for everyone to buy into and aspire to? If not, now is the time to create some.

Sell it

Your business should be structured for selling, whatever your plans, because then you will find growing and diversifying much easier. But I would be cautious whom you tell if you do plan to sell. The team may be dubious about company sales and mergers, often thinking that restructuring will cost them their jobs, which can cause a lot of unrest. Selling needs to be managed correctly and in phases, so timing is of the essence.

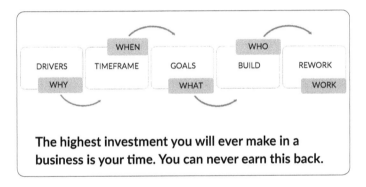

The highest investment you will ever make in a business is your time. You can never earn this back.

Ideally, you will have started your business with a view to selling, ensuring you achieve the maximum value for it. Remember your time investment in the business. Let's make it worth it.

When you are looking at making the business more appealing, the first port of call is simple: who will want to buy the business? For how much? A buyer's first worry may be that if the owner leaves, the business will falter. You might then have to enter into a workout clause, which can be draining and stressful. As much as you can, work towards making your business an 'off the shelf' offering, and start now. Then when the time comes, it will be easy to sell for maximum value.

You need to thrash this out, as this will give you the greatest chance of selling for the right amount of money (the right amount is whatever figure you need to take you to the next level – buying a different business, moving abroad, retiring etc). Sit down and work out exactly how much money you need. You may think the figure will be £10 million, for example, but when you work it out, you discover you only need £2–3 million. That may still sound daunting, but remember it is a total figure from zero. If you own a house worth £1 million and you owe £200,000, then you're already worth £800,000.

Once you know your ideal target/person for buying the business, shape the business and maximise the good points that your ideal buyer will want or need. What is your intellectual property? What is unique about your business and how can someone else increase the value of it? Is your target an individual? A competitor? An investor? If so, what are their criteria? Do you need to be top ten in the industry? Technology? Skills? Do you need to buy another business before you can sell yours? Now is the time to be asking all these questions, not when you're about to put your business up for sale.

Once you figure this out, you can look at getting a value for your business. Certain businesses are worth 1× earnings, others are 20× earnings. Where does yours lie?

Outside influences

These are the biggest drivers of immediate action. They can really focus the mind, as external pressures will usually give you a way of compromising to start with, then looking at the long term.

Generally poor health, yours or your life partner's, is top of the list of external pressures. If the chief executive has a debilitating illness or even passes, the business needs to have a two-stage process in place. The first stage covers the short-term running of the business, the second looks at its long-term stability and growth.

Poor health isn't the only outside influence. You may be driven by wanting to spend more time with family, or take more time away from the business for other personal reasons. Then there's a question of money. It may be called the root of all evil, but we all need money to allow us freedoms in life. Sometimes, the need to free up money can be urgent. For example, if something happens to your partner or children, you can suddenly find yourself needing ready access to money to cover the extra outgoings you have.

Other ventures/projects

You might be in a situation where you own more than one business, and there is one that drains more of your time than the others. You may decide to sell to someone or merge your business with another company (there's more on merging later in the chapter). Remember, no one wants to buy a lemon. Buyers will always go for the low-risk option, so make sure your business is the least risky on the market.

Moving geographically

The world is getting smaller. There is no reason why you cannot work from home, even in a different country. Modern technology is all around you to help with this. Why drive ten miles to a meeting when you can video chat? Why spend the time and money travelling when you can solve a lot of issues over the telephone or via email? Remember, your most important resource is time, and travelling can waste a lot of time.

There are literally thousands of tools to enable remote working. The systems you use today may not cope with how you want the business to run or how you and your team access the business, so now is a good time to upgrade or develop them. Many tools and systems have a low or zero entry cost, but over five years, they can become costly. Often investing money and/or time upfront can save you a lot more of those resources in the future. Be aware of companies increasing the costs. How much control will you have over this?

Merging the business

This can be make-or-break time in any business. Merging includes your company being taken over, a peer-to-peer merger, or you consuming the smaller business.

During a merger, you need your business to maintain its day-to-day running, while coping with changes, new processes and procedures. Beware: if the company you're acquiring is toxic, it can draw all your resources just to maintain it. Who knows the long-term impact this can have on the existing business?

A staged merger is often the best option. It may initially look to be costly, but staging the merger in timed chunks allows new managers to understand how the bigger company operates.

I recommend lots of due diligence on both sides of the merger. Sometimes things are covered up and figures can be over-exaggerated in the initial stages. Thorough due diligence saves a lot of heartaches in the future.

Fundamentally, you need to work out why you are looking at merging. Is it to scale the business faster? If so, which area are you currently failing to scale? Can you not scale by expanding sales or headhunting?

Look at a potential merger through the eyes of the other party. What is it about your business they will feel they have to have? Then build your business around this. The biggest fear for all parties in a merger is that by joining businesses together, they will bring down the whole house of cards.

Key takeaways

It is never too early to start planning for your exit from the business, no matter why you want to exit. Even if you currently have no intention of taking yourself out of the business, things change. In this chapter, we have looked at just a few of the things that may drive you to move on, including:

- Succession planning

- Selling the business

- Outside influences

- Other ventures

- Moving geographically

- Merging

You need to plan continually for that moment, so when it comes, even if it takes you by surprise, you're ready for it.

Now you have a clearer picture of what you want for your business and yourself, and when you want it. In the next section, we will pull everything together and start building towards your goals. Goals, after all, are just dreams – until you write them down!

PART THREE
WHAT

You've planned it, now achieve it.

5
Goals

You can have everything in the world you want. But you can't set life goals for other people, and you can't let other people set life goals for you.

Everyone needs life goals. If you don't know where you are heading, how will you know when you get there? This for me is the fun bit. You can go as crazy as you want – these are your goals, but it's important to get them down on paper. A written goal is four times more likely to be achieved than one in your head.

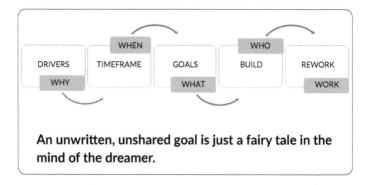

DRIVERS	TIMEFRAME	GOALS	BUILD	REWORK
WHEN		WHO		
WHY		WHAT		WORK

An unwritten, unshared goal is just a fairy tale in the mind of the dreamer.

There are lots of different ways of planning goals, and then presenting them. I like to break my goals down into three areas – business, personal and family. The most important, as a rule, is family, the biggest outside influencer, and then it's personal and lastly business. Then you need to add priorities to the business goals. Remember the business is what gives you the fuel (cash) for the personal stuff, but business should be fun, profitable and grow with you, so you need time and money goals, too.

Family goals are generally goals you share with a spouse, partner, parent, sibling etc, and may ultimately be driven by a desire to help others. For example, many people dream of buying their parents a big house or a world cruise. Then you build up your own personal goals.

If you already have written goals, that is a great start, but you possibly need to refocus them towards taking your time back from the business. Are the goals for your business focused on induction processes and team training manuals? These are the building blocks for all businesses.

How often do you look at the goals? Read them out loud? I generally suggest re-evaluating them every three to six months. Hopefully you will be ticking them off, possibly expanding them. For example, if you aimed at earning £100,000 a year, you may find you need to slide this up to £250,000 sooner than you expected.

Dream boards

If you are like me and are initially struggling with sorting and managing your goals, then dream boards can be a fun approach. I recommend you do this for yourself, your family, your partner and your kids, depending on their ages. If they are mid-teens, then perfect. They may dream of going to college and training to be a doctor, which may affect your financial goals. Stick their pictures on your dream boards.

My advice is to get some magazines (you can search Google Images, but this can be limited) and cut out pictures that represent the things you aspire to: a perfect beach holiday, a villa in Majorca, a supercar, a horse. Whatever it is, keep cutting out the pictures. They don't have to be exact representations; they just need to work as a stimulus. If a big house with a sweeping driveway and lots of land is your dream, don't hold back if you can't find the perfect photo. If it's time you crave, a random picture of a clock is all you need to get the grey matter ticking. The key is to make sure whatever you want is represented on the board.

Remember that goals do not all have to be huge, but they must stretch you. Whatever makes you tick. Goals *do not* have to be monetary. Money is rarely anyone's biggest driver, but money can enable you to set up an orphanage or support your local church. And if you're stuck, ask your nearest and dearest for ideas.

Once you have all your pictures, get a large piece of paper (A1 is best) and stick the pictures on it. I also have sayings and memory joggers on my dream board, printed in big letters. Put a date on the board, either the date you created it, or the goal dates. It really doesn't matter, as hopefully your goals will evolve in time. Then display it wherever you will see it regularly – I have mine next to my desk in my office. Your goals should be visible.

The first time you create a dream board, you may feel embarrassed. Don't be, just go for it. People love talking with me about my dream board, even though it was tongue in cheek to begin with. After a while, it started to excite me. Give it a try.

If you complete a family board, this can really help you understand your partner. If you think your goals are different, they may surprise you. Joining your dreams with other people's can be powerful. And the psychology behind a shared dream board means you will always hold each other accountable to stick 'the pin in the map'.

Timing

Always have timeframes on your major goals. If you do not, you might as well not write them down, as you are setting yourself up to fail. I'm not saying cut a finger off for every day you miss your target, but you will always get closer to achieving the dated goals than the ones without a date.

What timings are best to use? I generally break mine down into one-, three-, five- and ten-year goals. If you go any more than ten years, it is too far for the mind to focus on and the date doesn't have any effect. This is even a risk with ten-year goals, but you need to be realistic. The time you allocate depends on the size of the goal.

Perhaps start with the goal of owning your own home. There are two resources I recommend for this: *The Automatic Millionaire* by David Bach,[3] in which he breaks down some simple ways of reducing the time you're paying your mortgage in an easy, compound-

---

3   D Bach, *The Automatic Millionaire: A powerful one-step plan to live and finish rich* (Currency, 2016)

driven way, and a YouTube clip called 'The Position of Fuck You' by John Goodman.[4]

SMART goals and BHAGs

Having different length goals is vital: short- and long-term, personal and business. But what is important is that they are SMART:

- Specific

- Measurable

- Achievable

- Results orientated

- Time framed

SMART goals have been written about in self-help books for years, so goal setting is obviously a powerful process.

A big hairy audacious goal (BHAG)[5] is the time to go nuts. This is your guiding light, and it must be exciting. And if you can, share it.

---

4 'The Position of Fuck You' (John Goodman from *The Gambler*) [YouTube], 2015, www.youtube.com/watch?v=xdfeXqHFmPI

5 J Collins and J Porras, *Built to Last: Successful habits of visionary companies* (Random House Business, 2005)

CASE STUDY – THAT'S MY BHAG, BABY

A few years ago, I was interviewed for a newspaper. The reporter and I were discussing different business ventures I was involved in, how I'd got to where I was, and where I was heading. I explained to him that everyone should have a BHAG. I then explained what that was, and what mine was.

A few days later, I opened the newspaper to see my double-page spread under the headline 'My Ultimate Goal is to Sail my Own Yacht to the Monaco Grand Prix'. To this day, people still tell me about reading the story and ask how close to the goal I am.

Key points of a BHAG:

- It must be a massive stretch, even bigger than a triathlon, an ironman or the Marathon des Sables.

- It should really excite you when you read it – kid-in-a-sweet-shop time.

- It must have a completions date, for example 'by my fiftieth birthday'.

Bucket list

This has become a popular term. Most people know exactly what a bucket list is, they just don't actually write one down.

A bucket list is a really good way of feeling like you are going somewhere and accomplishing something. It is so easy to get your head down and work, not necessarily achieving the milestones you'd hoped to, or worse still, not even knowing what you're working for. A bucket list keeps you accountable and will make sure you achieve your milestones.

I'm sure you will agree that the older you get, the faster time passes. Here is a scary thought – the average person only starts going on real life-changing holidays when they reach the age of forty. You will find that your physical motivations have started to reduce by the age of sixty-five. What does this mean? It means you will probably only have twenty-five significant holidays. There are thousands of places to visit, but the average person will only see twenty-five.

I recommend that a holiday needs to be at least ten days, ideally two to three weeks, for you to unwind. A one-week holiday is just not enough. Make it your aim to have a two-week break every ninety days.

That said, you can add whatever you like to your bucket list, and you can add to it whenever you want. You can add small things like going to a trendy restaurant or seeing a show, or bigger goals like seeing the Northern Lights or walking the Great Wall of China. It really is up to you. The only rule is that you remove things that you genuinely do not want anymore, not the things you feel you won't achieve.

The great thing with being human is that everyone has their own beliefs, likes and dislikes. You can get on well with someone, but they may love Marmite and you (like me) may hate it. Often people describe their loved one's foibles as being the things they miss most about that person.

The things that drove you as a child can come out when you're creating your bucket list. When you ask yourself why you didn't pursue this dream or that, it brings up responses that the 'sensible' you would normally shrug off.

I have seen this with men (it's usually men) who get to a certain age and finally take the plunge and buy a sports car or a soft top. Their eyes light up and they are back to being a child in a toyshop again. Is this not what life is all about?

When you are indulging in a bit of retail therapy, it is not the thing you are buying that matters, it's how it makes you feel. There is a great scene in the animation film *Ratatouille* where the food critic tastes the ratatouille that the rat has cooked, and is instantly taken back to the feeling he had as a child. Your dreams need to do this.

Hard work = rewards

All goals need to get your mind thinking in this way. If you want a yacht, plan and invest, sow the seed and eventually reap the rewards.

My goal with this book is to get you to where you want to go, and give you the time to truly enjoy it when you get there. What is the point of busting a gut to buy a yacht, then not having the time to use it? Or worse still, being too old by then to enjoy it fully.

You need to get to the big stuff, but achieve the smaller stuff first. And when you do achieve it, it's important to give yourself a reward. If you hit a sales/growth figure, reward yourself. A meal in a restaurant, a new watch – it really doesn't matter, as long as it is important to you and your mind registers it as a reward. It's like the lollipop you got as a child for being well behaved for the dentist.

Lots of small rewards are for your general targets and goals. You can easily share these with your family and/or team. Remember, a reward may seem small, but it's the significance of it that counts.

Mid-size rewards are for achieving longer-term goals. This will be a holiday or new car for something that stretches you. When you achieve it, you deserve a good reward.

Then there's the big stuff. This will be a three-month tour along Route 66 or a supercar, something you can go wild for when you have achieved those BHAGs.

Rewards are important. If you reach a goal and don't get rewarded, this can have a negative effect. You will not get as excited about reaching the next goal. Remember, passion drives us all. If the reward when you get there is not as good as you dreamed, you might take your foot off the gas.

Team goals and rewards

Do not forget your team! The people around you are going to help you get to where you want to go, and more importantly, keep you there. You must come up with rewards for them, too.

Some industries need monetary rewards. You must pay good bonuses in banking, for example, otherwise the best people will leave. But for a group (an entire team), the real power is the feeling of being part of something big. If you all set out on a 'journey' (I hate using this word, so I apologise) to reach the summit, it's important to celebrate together, whether it is a staff party, lunch, bowling. Often a great idea is a barbecue where the management does all the cooking and serving. Whatever the reward, make sure you enjoy it together as a team.

You could use magic numbers as goals around your workplace or on your company's intranet (internal website), whatever suits your work environment. You need to get the team in on these numbers, though. They might be for your net promoter score (NPS) – I would highly recommend reading *The Ultimate Question* by Reichheld and Markey[6] on this subject – a daily sales figure or a number of new customers. There is no right or wrong, but it is important that all team members are behind the numbers. If they own the numbers, they will aspire to beat them. And a little intercompany competition can be good.

Just be careful that magic numbers are used in the right way and not seen as pressure tactics. This is why I highly recommend getting the team involved in coming up with the numbers. It can be powerful to have a day away from the normal work environment to thrash these out and inspire people.

SIDE NOTE – PERSONAL BEST DRIVES THE INDIVIDUAL

The team members should all have their own personal best figures, rather than a random sales target the management have come up with. They will then strive to beat their personal best because they know it is achievable and will be playing to their profile.

---

6   F Reichheld and B Markey, *The Ultimate Question 2.0: How net promoter companies thrive in a customer-driven world* (Harvard Business Press, 2011)

Plan how you want to be

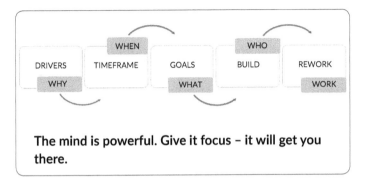

DRIVERS	TIMEFRAME	GOALS	BUILD	REWORK
WHEN	WHO
WHY		WHAT		WORK

The mind is powerful. Give it focus – it will get you there.

Your goals should always be how you ultimately want to be. You don't plan to be OK, then the next day plan to be a bit better. Come up with the ideal and don't stop until you get there. Then when you do, start planning and striving for more. This is a never-ending process, and is fundamental to building a profitable enterprise that runs without you. But the ultimate goal is a profitable enterprise that *grows* without you. Imagine how powerful 1,000 minds are. Give all your team members focus and they will get you there faster.

Here the six types of mastery a person can seek:

- Personal
- Professional
- Physical
- Emotional

- Spiritual

- Mental

Make sure that your goals and your company's goals mean something to the people around you. To do this, a goal should satisfy at least two if not more of the types of mastery.

Have you ever been to a sales presentation or a company meeting where the financial or managing director tries to supercharge the people with targets and how the figures looked for last year and project for the coming year? How boring is this for the majority of the audience? I am not saying that you shouldn't use figures – remember people want to be part of a winning team/business, so it's good if your results are growing – but you need to get them focused on the six types of mastery. Make them feel they are making a difference, a change. Few people are driven by numbers and most don't want their egos massaged; they just want to follow a worthy cause.

Decide on your actions, goals and plans, and really get the team on board. If they don't buy in, you will find it an uphill battle to achieve your goals. Or there will be false enthusiasm to begin with, but this will dwindle within weeks.

A really good way of getting the team to buy in is to get them to come up with the goals, while you and your executive team guide them. Really delve into why they work for your business. What drives them? Remember, people will usually say money, but this is never the real reason. Most people can move employers to get more money; there is always a higher purpose.

Get the team to write their goals down and explain what they would like the company to achieve. Also get their ideas on improvements. Open up the discussion. A great way to do this is to get them to take turns to be the boss and say, 'If I was in charge, I would...' You may be amazed at the varying viewpoints. This can be a real eye opener.

If you know where you are heading with crystal clarity, you can then guide your team to focus on the right things. If your team is digging a road, what is the first thing to do? Mark which direction it will go in. The road might be so long that you can't even see the end, but if the team knows where it is going, they can follow it. Then as they get near to where your markings end, you extend the goals.

A mistake people make is to get charged up with goals and write them everywhere, but within a few months, the momentum has died and the same goals stay on the walls. After a while, people stop noticing they are there. Make sure your goals are constantly refreshed and keep the teams accountable.

Key takeaways

Goals, from the small to the huge and audacious, need to be owned by everyone in the business. And for this, they must have buy-in.

There are a number of ways to create and develop your goals, many of which we have covered in this chapter:

- Make sure all goals are written down – a written goal is four times more likely to be achieved than an unwritten one.

- Use dream boards to help you visualise what you are striving for.

- Make your goals SMART, and have a few BHAGs thrown in to get you excited.

- Create a bucket list.

- Reward yourself and your team for getting to a goal.

Now you have the written plan of how the business will evolve over the coming years, you need to bring all the pieces of the puzzle together. Make sure your goals drive the business. Momentum is the key – once you start moving and the big motivation takes over, nothing will be getting in your way.

6
Structure – The Pieces Of The Puzzle

The question that plagues so many business owners is: 'Will it all come crashing down without me?' Let's find out.

Now that we have discussed the goals of the business, we need to look at all the pieces in the puzzle to make sure they can run on their own while supporting and helping the other pieces. This is the fundamental issue with most companies – they can't.

All companies, regardless of size, have different departments. Some smaller companies will have all departments in the same office, or even the same people wearing two different hats for different departments. If the people in the sales and growth side are not in sync with the base of the business (production and accounts), all too frequently the whole deck of cards comes tumbling down. Companies all around the world fail for the same reason: they are not able to cope with growth and simply run out of cash (not profit).

You need to be careful this does not happen to your company.

Where are you now?

Where are you today? This is the most important step towards being the architect of a successful business that grows and prospers without you. That said, you need to be relaxed and open about it – there are no right or wrong ways of doing this.

I suggest doing this task alone to begin with. Generally, I like working in groups as it gives a much more non-biased outcome, but this first part is where you really need to look at how you visualise the business. You will open this to the team at the next stage. For now, keep it simple, but make sure you do it!

Get a large piece of paper, write your company name in a circle in the centre of the page, then draw five lines coming from the circle. These are for the five departments all businesses have. Write them close to the circle in the middle as you will flare off from them.

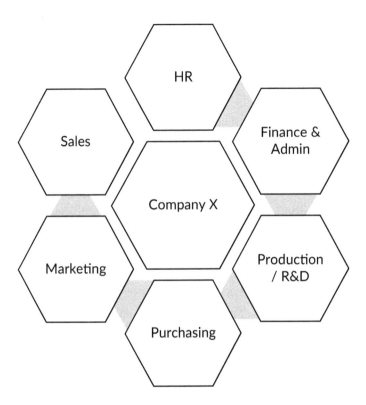

The five departments are (you may give them differ-ent names, but essentially they are the same):

- Human resources – this department needs the most training. It directs where your business is heading through recruitment, inductions, health and safety, unions etc.

- Finance and admin – this is the department looking after the money throughout the business. It's key to keeping the business going through reports and working with the other departments.

- Production/research and development – this generates the products and/or services the business produces at the right price and in a timely manner.

- Purchasing – this department buys all the raw materials and general items to ensure the company runs smoothly.

- Sales and marketing – this is what drives the cash into the business, through selling to customers, advertising and giving the business its character in the outside world.

All companies need these five departments in one shape or form. You may have a small purchasing department if you are in the services sector, or if you're in manufacturing, this could be a large department. Either way, it keeps the business going at a grass-roots level.

You now need to note what the departments currently do and how many staff each has. If you have a business of more than fifty people, then just name the department and list its main activities. That will be sufficient for the exercise – keep it simple. List what each department does in as few words as possibly. We want your mind working, so speed is imperative. Get it down on paper.

You can use different colours if you find it easier to break down and understand. The key is to be honest and stick to exactly what the business is today. No planning allowed – not at this stage. Remember, you need to know where you are today before you prepare for tomorrow.

Once you have completed this exercise, take two magic markers/felt-tip pens in bright colours and mark each area that you are currently involved in. What is involvement? There are two stages:

1. You have an active role working in the department at least once a week.

2. You have an active say in what happens in the department, but it is largely run without you, except for… It can be anything, even simply signing the cheque, but you need to know what this is so you can manage your way out completely.

Now you can see at a high level what your involvement is in your company. But it is crucial you are 100% honest. The critical question in all of this is: 'Could I have six months away from the business and everything would be fine, if not better, on my return?'

Realistic planning

There are two things that you need to do to get you out of the business, depending on its size and the legal entity. If you have a large business with a board and shareholders, you will need to justify your position within the business. Fundamentally, though:

- Do you need to restructure the business to allow for your exit?

- Do you need to grow the business before you can exit?

If it is the first option, your planning can be about training and coaching the team to get you out of the pivotal role within the business. If you have recently been appointed into the position, then this can be a great exercise to look clearly at what is happening beneath your feet.

If it is the latter, then you need to get three phases completed. Decide on when each will happen, but let's take a total of five years as an example. Plan the structure of the company towards what it will look like in five years' time.

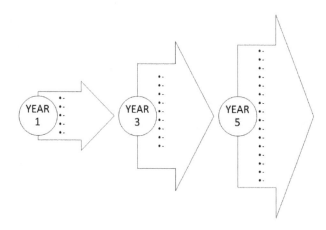

This can be a great exercise to complete with a pencil, so you can adjust as you go. Remember, these are your goals and targets for the structure of your business. You are free to go as big or as detailed as you like, but they may need refining in the future.

Step one. Make sure your business is fully scalable; don't build a company that has individuals solely responsible. Always remember your end goal. If it is to sell, will you be selling the company as a whole? Do you service more than one niche market? If so, do you need each branch of the business to be able to run separately under one umbrella? You might find that these can be broken away in stages.

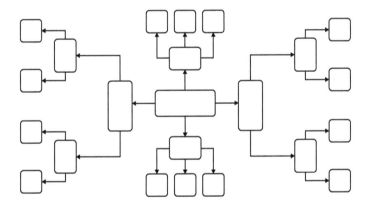

Another strategy is to grow separate branches of your business, and then sell them off one at a time to raise finance for the main bulk of the business. This can create a real buzz around the executive team, as many are likely to find themselves running their own companies under the overarching business.

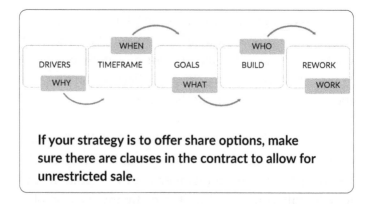

	WHEN		WHO	
DRIVERS	TIMEFRAME	GOALS	BUILD	REWORK
WHY		WHAT		WORK

If your strategy is to offer share options, make sure there are clauses in the contract to allow for unrestricted sale.

Step two. When you have completed step one (it usually takes half a day, maximum a full day), go through your plans with your management team. This is important as you will not be the main driving force behind the plans, they will. You may decide to go through it with a couple first, depending on the size of your company, but I would recommend one of them being on the finance side.

The reason for this is to know how much turnover you will need to be able to employ the teams of people the business will require. I am not saying you need a full projections report for every aspect – this type of structure is not about that. It is more so you understand that adding fifty people to the sales team will mean an extra £20 million on the bottom line to fulfil all the extra business, so the structure must support this. Sometimes it's easy to get carried away, so it is good to have someone in the accounts department to bring you back down to reality. This also gives the plan depth – if the numbers stack up, then what is stopping it from coming true?

Step three. Once you have come up with your planned structures for the coming years, put them into a format that everyone can understand. Remember, you need clarity for the future of your business. I like to use organisational charts for this, because they are easy to understand and you don't need the exact detail. You can just name the positions and the people involved in them.

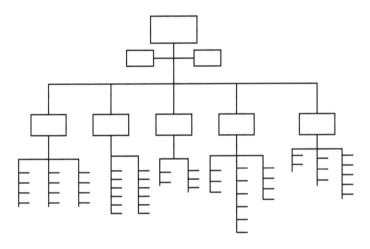

This enables everyone in your teams to understand your plans for the future of the business. It is your job to decide how much you divulge; some business owners will show all the stages of their plan, allowing people to get on board, others are sceptical about being so transparent. I would possibly choose not to publish all of them.

One thing that is certain is the HR and accounts departments need to have a detailed view of the plan. All the decisions involving recruiting and training must use these departments as a sounding board. When recruiting new team members, you need these departments to make sure they have the focus and are positioned in the correct way. Get the momentum pushing in the right direction from the beginning.

Sharing the structure and plan leads to something else all businesses need: accountability.

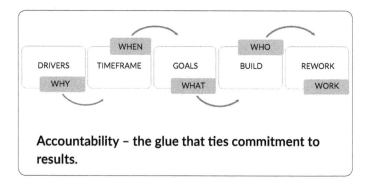

Accountability – the glue that ties commitment to results.

Being accountable to someone or something is powerful. Our lives, both business and personal, need to have purpose and often the best way to achieve this is through accountability. For a position in your company to generate the self-motivation to achieve, the employee needs to have as many people holding them accountable as possible.

Life is all too easy. We can just sit back when we get to a certain place in our lives, such as being promoted, buying a house or achieving a status. To really reach for the stars, you need to lay it out there. Tell everyone your goal for the structure and size of the business, and go for it!

Positioning the company

When you know how your company will look in the future, there is no better time to examine its positioning. So how do you do this? There are a few things that will make its positioning powerful.

Firstly, especially when you're looking to sell, position yourself and your business from the prospective buyer's point of view. Do not build a business that is only fit for a sole trader. A company or a person looking to buy, build or sell will have certain criteria they feel the business has to run with, so don't pigeonhole yourself. You may even end up getting interest from a competitor if you position your business with the buyer in mind.

Then write a for-sale advert for your business, breaking what the business does down into fifty words or fewer. This is a great exercise for trimming the fat that doesn't add any value to the services or products you offer. So many companies are afraid of turning away business, so they complete tasks for clients that actually lose them money or, worse, their reputation. It is better to look at strategic alliances where you can outsource or even give the business to a competitor. If you know your market, then others will understand it too.

Your positioning must set you apart. It is difficult to do this in many staple industries, but as much as you can, look for your unique selling point. Imagine you were looking at investing in a company. You decide on the sector, then you look for companies within the sector. What would you look for? What would make one stand out from another? Believe it or not, it is pretty much that simple.

Finally, you must be prepared to make sacrifices; you cannot be all things to all people. This will just convey that you have no true direction. Great businesses focus on the single customer, creating their offerings around that person. Never build a business around a product; these change over time, but the customer's needs and wants do not change so fast. Focus on one thing, go with that, and get the team and the prospective new owners to buy into it.

Everything about positioning is for the long term, so there are no short cuts. If you are unsure how the business needs to look, do some research internally into deals that have happened in the past three to five years. Generally any longer ago than that, they cease to be relevant. A good investment is to employ a consultant and/or firm that specialises in the selling of a business. They will be able to give you the complete picture on what prospective buyers are looking for.

Completing a detailed top-down view of the business map is reassuring for your teams. If they feel you are preparing to sell, this can be unnerving, but if you are rebuilding/restructuring the business ready for growth, then the team will get behind this.

We are all creatures of habit – people love and trust consistency. Does anyone go to McDonald's for the quality of the food or the top-class service? No, the reason this chain is so successful is because it is consistent the world over. You know you will get the same hamburger wherever you are in the world.

It is worth mentioning at this point what the people buying a business look for as their number-one priority with regards to you selling up. Although they will rarely admit it, they are looking for the least risky takeover where their investment will be safe. They do not want to be responsible for buying a business that will cost them or their company time and resources.

If you think buyers go for the most amazing opportunities, they do not. They go for the safest option that ticks most of the right boxes, so you need to make sure, if you're reshaping your business, you do it from an outsider's perspective. Create a company that can be run by anyone, because the cogs are so well oiled.

Know the numbers

Now that you have the company mapped out in front of you and you know how you would like it to look, sit down with the bean counters. This is not only from a 'Can we afford it?' perspective, but also from a reporting and managing point of view, which is key and will be unique to every business.

You need to look at how each department runs and the KPIs around that department. Then you ask who needs to know the exact numbers from the department and how the department will react with the numbers. Remember, the business must react according to the numbers it is generating. The marketing department will have KPIs in place, but these are directly governed by sales that will reflect on the bottom line. You need to make sure these interlink, so take each department and look at what the KPIs deliver.

The objective is to run the whole business from a single sheet of paper. It is incredible how many businesses produce pages of numbers and graphs, but don't use them to seek improvement. And bear in mind that this is often the hardest area to support, and then move away from. Remember, business owners tend to be worried that no one will drive the business like they do.

With your company structure in front of you, the fun can commence. This is when dreams can really become reality. Who can take over the different tasks that you do? Make a list of the people and put a date next to each task to say when you will have delegated it.

Often business owners look at their successor as taking over the reins. This may be true, but you need to make sure your tasks are covered by someone, and covered by someone else in their absence. This is what really adds value when you're selling the business. If you take yourself out of the business, but load everything you do onto one person, the prospective buyer will just see that person as a potential bottleneck.

Looking at the KPIs allows you to consider where the company wastes money and how it can lean up the operation. I am not necessarily talking about cutting staff, but you may want to adjust people's roles.

Get another piece of paper (or use a tablet or computer). Draw two equally spaced lines down the page. On the left-hand column, write 'Departments' at the top. At the top of the centre column, write: 'Activity/ Task', and at the top of the right-hand column, write: 'Insource/Outsource/Maybe'.

Now look at all the tasks and functions that your business needs to run. Do you need to do them all internally or could you outsource some? There are only two questions to ask when completing this:

- Does the role have to be done by an internal person? If so, why (eg the business needs total control over the task or for security reasons)?

- Which is more financially viable, doing the task internally or outsourcing, and does outsourcing offer better skills and training? A specialist advertising agency, for example, would have far more experience than internal marketers.

When you're doing this exercise, always look at which option adds the most value for the end user. All too often, people look at cutting costs, and customer support suffers somewhere down the line as a result.

If you have a successful business with you at the helm, you need to be clear on why it is successful and what people like about you and your business. Then keep this in mind when you're looking at reshaping and restructuring your business. Do not lose the seemingly trivial things that may be what makes the difference to the individuals who choose to use your company over others. Remember that change is all too easy. If you have a loyal customer base, do not under any circumstances jeopardise this.

It's time to delegate

Now you (hopefully) have a long list of things you are responsible for, look strategically at getting the weight of responsibility from you and onto the shoulders of others. Nordstrom, an American department store, is an excellent example of empowering all staff with one single rule: 'Use best judgement in all situations'. What a great atmosphere this generates. How can you create this type of culture?

Delegation is a slow process. It should never be rushed, and make sure it is done correctly. Do not just dump everything on whoever walks into your office next and expect them to run the entire business.

How can you delegate best? First, break each task down into what you do, then ask why you do it. Do you do it well? Who can do it better?

Then create a step-by-step manual for all the tasks. This is fundamental, as it will lead to a steady and sure process of moving responsibilities away from you. You can get others to create the manuals, but it is important to have an active role in making sure they are detailed and correct. You are the one who knows the quirky bits of each task.

For example, there might be a glitch in some software that means you have to login using different credentials, or sometimes the reports are estimated. Whatever the details are, you must document them.

You also want to eliminate the risk of people stealing your time. The less detail you have, the more they will ask you for help. This is wasted time that you can never get back.

Writing manuals is a great way of looking at stream-lining processes. If you have a task that is low value but takes a long time, is there a way of automating it? If you pay someone £200 a month to do a job that you could automate with the right software for £150 per month, and it would probably do the job more quickly and efficiently, then this is a worthwhile investment. There are lots of free or relatively low-cost flowchart software templates available, for example. You can even hand draw a chart and get someone else to create it – Fixer is good for this. Or you could create videos around all processes.

It is incredible how small tasks can expand and become laborious, until someone looks at altering these processes. Do you have any 'this is how we've always done it' tasks that continue to be used every day? Get rid of as many bottlenecks and laborious tasks as possible.

SIDE NOTE – GO PAPERLESS

Do you waste time printing out invoices that are emailed to you? There are two ways of fixing this.

Go paperless and store the invoice from the screen in a relevant folder and/or use specialist software. There is a lot of such software available, but make sure what you decide to use syncs directly with your accountancy package.

For about £30, you can buy an Outlook add-on that prints the attachment when an invoice comes in and puts the email into a folder of your choice. This saves on average thirty minutes every day for a company receiving ten invoices a day.

The real key is to shift your thinking. Every time you do something (and I mean every time), either write an instruction in your evolving manual or list all the manuals you need to make in a spreadsheet. Once you get into the flow of doing this, it will accelerate your exit, especially when you start reaping the rewards of more free time. When you are stamping out mutual mystification, the written word is gospel.

If you delegate tasks by showing someone how to do them without a manual for them to use when you are not there, they will inevitably make mistakes, start doing the tasks in a different way, or worse, let the quality slip. True delegation will result in the task being done the same way consistently, every time.

Human nature is to avoid looking stupid. People may ask you for help a couple of times after you have shown them how to do a task, but if they are still not 100% sure, they will just muddle along. This is where consistency and quality can pay the price.

Your rules of the game

You cannot discipline anyone who has (in your eyes) done something wrong if they were not given clear written instructions to begin with. This is why people enjoy playing sports. They know what the overall objective is – score a goal or get points – and the rules add detail, like what constitutes a foul or cheating. This level of detail is what you need for your business.

The first step is to know what the goal is for each individual department. For example:

- Production may want quality and defects goals.

- Sales may want a numeric figure to achieve or to beat others.

- Marketing may look at market share or an overall reach figure.

- HR may focus on an NPS score.

Remember that no one can get excited about the numbers alone. You need to give them a guiding light, which is why the goal is so important.

Then you add in boundaries and guidelines, which cover pretty much everything from the times employees should be working, to the attitude they should have and their overall behaviour in the workplace with colleagues and superiors. This may sound quite strict, but it is more about allowing people to grow and flourish in an environment that everyone can be happy in. Rules and boundaries mean people feel safe to give their body and soul, be enthused by the work they are doing and the company they work for, and not just turn up and collect their wages.

Say honesty is at the heart of your company. If someone is stealing clients from competitors using underhand methods, this needs to be addressed, but if the team member doesn't know this is not acceptable, then what is to stop them? What is to stop this practice becoming commonplace?

There need to be boundaries and rules in everything we do. For example, how much fun would playing golf be if there was no limit to the number of holes? It would probably get tedious after eight hours or so of play. Exactly the same applies in business – everything needs boundaries and rules.

The question to ask is: 'Do people in my business know what they are supposed to do?' If there is any doubt, then I suggest looking into your induction process (we will be covering this in Chapter 8). Does everyone know what your company is looking for from each department and role?

For many companies, it is just a numbers game. The more numbers, the merrier, but is this the most profitable course? If you are selling a product, this may not be relevant, but in the services sector it is important to grade your clients. A-grade clients are not just the ones who pay the most, they also treat your team well and value you and your service offering. Once you have your ideal A-grade clients, make sure the sales team know who they are.

Home or abroad?

In this final part of the chapter, let's discuss the structure of the company if you want to stay at the helm, but run it from a distance. This mainly means ensuring people within the team understand their place and how they fit in. It is often harder to assert your authority if you are mainly communicating via email or telephone.

The place we need to start is with security. Make sure your business is secure from the inside. Your employees might seem to love you now, but what if they leave and click 'delete all' on their way out?

What you need is to bring everyone on board and get them flourishing and raring to go, but there will always be people who step out of line, so make sure you protect your company against this. It amazes me how many companies do not use the built-in security within their software. It can be a laborious job to set it up, but it's worthwhile in the long term.

The bare minimum to look at is what people can and can't access, or more importantly, what they are able to read and write. It can be too easy for a disgruntled member of the team to delete data or copy the database and take it with them to a competitor. Also, look at what people are able to export. It has been known to cripple companies if data gets into the wrong hands.

I would recommend investing in software that is accessible from anywhere and is thoroughly backed up at least daily, if not every second. If you are working a distance from the main office, you need to minimise the chance of disasters. Make sure you have a clear disaster recovery process documented. In today's technology age, there is absolutely no reason to have any doubt in your technology and the data behind it.

You also need to look at the tasks you will be doing if you are moving away. It is important that all tasks are covered, so keep firmly in mind that what you are doing now is a temporary measure and soon someone else will be doing those tasks.

Really adjust your thinking on this. Everything you do has to be set out in a manual, so that anyone can do it (within reason).

Key takeaways

The question that plagues so many business owners is: 'Will it all come crashing down without me?' In this chapter, we have been putting the structures in place to make sure you never have to worry about this:

- Plan what the business will look like, and note where it is now.

- Look at whether you need to restructure or grow the business before you exit.

- Position your business to appeal to prospective buyers – what is your unique selling point?

- Look at your KPIs to see what tasks can be trimmed. Is doing a task internally really the best option, or could it be automated or outsourced?

- Delegate, delegate, delegate! But make sure you have detailed everything you do in manuals before you do so.

- Put in place clear rules and boundaries so everyone can feel safe in the workplace to give their all.

- Decide where you will run your company from if you want to step back, but remain involved. Do you have the processes and security in place for your teams to manage without you?

This is really where things start to change for everyone associated with the business. Your teams will have seen changes, certainly your management team will, but as things move forward, you need to make sure you have the right people in place. In the next section, we will explore how to recruit you out of the business.

PART FOUR
WHO

You can't do it alone.

7
Team

Your team will ultimately either get you to your goal or bring the house down. Simple.

Let's not overcomplicate things. The team with the best players wins, so you recruit and retain the best players. No matter what industry you are in, if you have the best players, you can share and absorb learning with everyone around you.

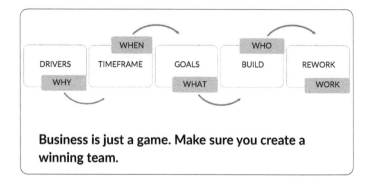

Business is just a game. Make sure you create a winning team.

The right people

When a business of any size is successful, it is all about the people, not the money. You cannot impress or dishearten a computer; a building will not feel inferior if it's smaller than the one next to it.

'Practise what you preach' is important throughout a business. Get the feeling right, and you will fly. Get it wrong and you will hit the ground, hard! Most companies get some of it right, so they hover. They're in flight, but will not reach their true potential.

You need to nurture the human element around your business. Any company, from a sole trader on a market stall to the largest organisation in the world, needs to appreciate that every aspect of human interaction is important.

I have broken the people involved in a company down into three categories:

- The people you serve (the market you're in/your customers)

- Your business partners and associates (suppliers, investors, stakeholders)

- The team you build (your employees)

In the context of this chapter, we will focus solely on the third category, but much of the content can be relevant to the first two as well. Let's start by finding out if you have got the right people on your bus.

You can do this exercise yourself, or get your managers and executives to do it if they are more connected to the individuals than you are. Imagine you have the opportunity to fire and rehire your staff with no negative impact or liability. Who would you be happy to rehire? Who do you feel is a real asset to the team and company as a whole?

Hopefully the list of people you wouldn't be happy to rehire is small, but if you have a big list, then you might need to delve into whether the issues are really the individuals or an underperforming manager. For the purpose of this exercise, write down why you would not rehire certain people. Quick bullet points are fine, but don't make it personal. 'I don't like him or her' isn't a good enough reason; ask yourself what it is you do not like. Is it their attitude? Are they disrespectful?

Once you have answered these questions, you can focus on training these people. You can either train them to be better suited to your organisation or so they jump off the bus, but either way, you need to be crystal clear on what you expect of them and how their past behaviour has no place within the culture of the business. The funny thing about this is that most people won't realise how their actions have impacted the business.

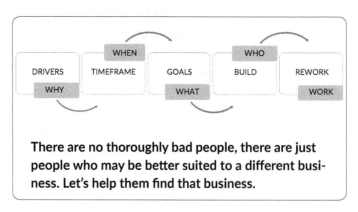

There are no thoroughly bad people, there are just people who may be better suited to a different business. Let's help them find that business.

If you prefer more structure to this process, you might like to grade the team, especially if you are delegating this task to management. Obviously, you need to be careful how you approach this; you can't call it a 'sack 'em or keep 'em' exercise. A performance review tends to work well, but remember to keep it emotionless with zero bias. If you are asking personalised questions, you will find different managers will grade in different ways, so give them examples to follow.

Here are five examples of areas to measure. On a scale of one to ten, with ten being excellent and one being awful, how does the team member score on:

- Attendance

- Punctuality

- Being a team player

- Having similar beliefs to the organisation

- Willingness to accept change

Then, ask if the company could manage without each team member. If it could, why is that? Does a person need more training? If so, in what areas? It is important that you complete this exercise so you can move to the next stage and decide if you need to recruit.

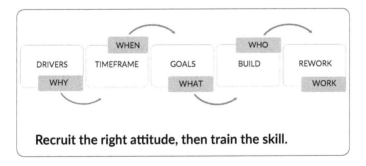

Recruit the right attitude, then train the skill.

If people are retiring, make sure you don't just recruit for the same position. Always look at the business structure and take the opportunity to separate a role or add to an existing role.

Once you know what you think of the team, you need to find out what they think of you, the management and company as a whole. Ask every single person within the company two simple things:

- On a scale of one to ten, how likely would you be to recommend working for this company to a friend?

- Write five words that you feel describe the company (you can give examples to help shape your business).

If your employees feel aligned and loyal to the company, you can guarantee the customers will too. It is not enough to pay people a wage and tell them to get on with it. We are all humans, and humans need a purpose.

You must understand your teams' value as you can't run your business without them. Retaining great people and customers is the way forward, so when you're looking at shaping the company from the ground up, ask:

- Who will take over from you?

- Will there be more than one who takes over?

- Will people become departments?

- Do you need to outsource any of the departments?

Stephen Covey in his book *The 7 Habits of Highly Effective People*[7] talks about the emotional bank account, ie the amount of trust that has been built up in a relationship. Successful leaders realise they cannot constantly make withdrawals from this account; they must make deposits too. The aim is always to create a win-win scenario; each person involved should gain from the situation. Another great book on this subject is *How Full Is Your Bucket?*[8]

It can be a great leveller when you put your team members through their paces and effectively ask them to do more than the standard job that is required of them. You will be adjusting how people work, and they may have been doing the job the same way for thirty years, so you need to manage this carefully and nurture the changes through. Replenish their bucket, or make a deposit in the emotional bank account. Otherwise their bottom-line output will suffer, and the whole reason for doing this is so their bottom-line output increases through them wanting it too.

Now we've looked at the importance of the team, let's start planning for getting the changes happening. How will you rally the troops?

7   S R Covey, *The 7 Habits of Highly Effective People: Powerful lessons in personal change* (Simon & Schuster, 1990)
8   T Rath and D O Clifton, *How Full Is Your Bucket? Positive strategies for work and life* (Gallup, 2013)

A communications company

Communication is the one thing that we as humans find either easy or a complete mystery. Have you ever spoken with someone about their relationship and discovered they shy away from discussing things because they don't think their partner will understand, or they say it's easier just to get on with it? This is exactly what you cannot have within a business.

The lines of communication need to be wide open. If they are not, then you might hit a bump that turns into a mountain. Communication is key to a successful long-term strategy; the issues will not become apparent today, this month or even this year, but at some point, they will.

First and foremost, you need to tell everyone about the changes, explain your why for the business and hope they will follow you. Whatever you do, do *not* express the why in financial terms. Share your guiding light, and hopefully your people will be attracted and guided by the same.

Do not tell them your personal why behind the changes (so you can retire to the Caribbean, for example). The why needs to make the company solid, sustainable and give everyone stability so they work towards a shared goal. Everyone wants to be on the winning team of the number-one company. A powerful why gives a team purpose far more than numbers ever will – the Caribbean holiday will be the by-product.

How will you communicate your why? I am a great believer in daily meetings, but not laborious ones that take hours. Aim to have short, sharp, punchy meetings that are structured and get straight to the point (and keep the rhythm of the business flowing).

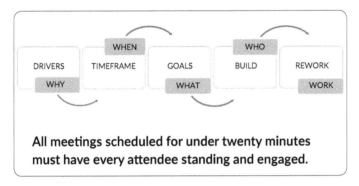

All meetings scheduled for under twenty minutes must have every attendee standing and engaged.

Tailor your meetings for your business and each department within that business, but I recommend the maximum number of people present is eight as everyone needs to have an active role within the meeting. More than eight attendees usually results in meetings running over.

CASE STUDY – SYN-STAR

At one of my companies, Syn-Star, we have different templates for each day of the week. This enables the meetings to flow freely. It also stops people questioning what they are doing and why they are doing it.

People do not need to know everything, or discuss the same project every day, but on a weekly basis we may decide to go into a bit more detail. Some basic elements that we cover in our meetings at Syn-Star are (I have put rough timings next to each):

- What each attendee has planned for the day (thirty-five to forty seconds per person)
- What internal repairs and jobs are in process (three minutes max)
- Any quotations needed (twenty seconds)
- Any bottlenecks (any project they're stuck on or delays – one minute)
- What work has carried over from the previous day or week (one minute)
- Business lunches planned (thirty seconds)
- Monthly theme (examples of – one minute)
- Numbers from previous day/week/month (one minute)
- Golden rules/values to read to the team (different person picked every day – one minute)
- Praise/issues/values, any other business (one minute)

There are other things that are more specific, but crucially, we can get through the meeting within twenty minutes.

It's important that different people run the meeting each time; it should never always be the manager. This engages everyone and creates a much purer environment. A great book on this subject is *Scaling Up* by Verne Harnish.[9]

Communication can really change the direction of the business, but it does take a few months for people to get behind it. You will probably get more kickback from a complete change in your employees' daily routines than anything else, but stay committed to it. Communication gets them talking about the change, understanding it and explaining it to each other.

Meetings

Monthly themes are golden. Plan them around feedback from employee and customer surveys. My advice is to make them fun and different, and they can really keep the mood upbeat. Don't focus on negatives, but sometimes negative examples can be worth discussing.

Here are a few examples of monthly themes:

- Processes – the way you use them to generate trust and increase the customer experience.

- Upsell/cross sell – examples of how teams have executed these.

- Changes to improve – what have you done differently to improve something?

---

9   V Harnish, *Scaling Up*

- Helping others, because they would do the same for you.

- Going above and beyond in customer service.

- Working well with your teammates.

- What has been finished and checked?

- Numbers and measurements – measurements to aim higher.

- Onwards and upwards – learning to be better.

- Finding and keeping customers.

- Finding better ways to do things.

Weekly meetings can be relevant, but you will find daily meetings can cover most things. It is highly dependent on the business you are in and how the company is structured. You may possibly want to break meetings down into departments, or even just managers. What you do not want to do is overlap the monthly meetings, as these are generally important, high level and broad range. Make sure they always have future actions.

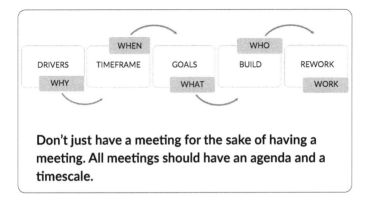

Don't just have a meeting for the sake of having a meeting. All meetings should have an agenda and a timescale.

Your time, and everyone else's, is important, and meetings that cover all aspects of the business can tend to drag on if not managed in a timely fashion. Depending on the situation your business is in, you can fluctuate the time that each person gets to speak at a meeting. So if you are implementing a lean production process, for example, the production side of the business will probably need more face time, or the accounts department if it is implementing new software.

Monthly meetings are important. They are your high-level snapshot of what is happening within the business. All monthly meetings must:

- Cover the entire business through one-page reports (remember not to bore everyone with a thirty-page report)

- Allow each person a fair amount of time to talk, but no more than fifteen minutes each, including questions and answers

- Have a template for the meetings to follow

- Include goals and targets within the reports:

  - What the goal was set at

  - Did you achieve the goal?

  - Reasons for hitting or missing the goal

- Clarify for each attendee what the purpose of their report is

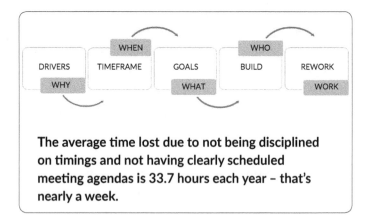

| DRIVERS | TIMEFRAME | GOALS | BUILD | REWORK |

WHEN — WHO

WHY — WHAT — WORK

The average time lost due to not being disciplined on timings and not having clearly scheduled meeting agendas is 33.7 hours each year – that's nearly a week.

The outcome of the meeting can be shaped into a one-page document containing all the relevant figures and results. This is probably the most important part of the meeting. Remember your goal is to run the business and understand how it is performing from a single sheet of paper.

You might find to begin with that the report is three to four pages. See how much detail you require in the report and reduce it down. This will depend on how fast your company is growing and expanding.

Key takeaways

The team with the best players wins, so make sure your staff are the best players. But how do you do that?

- Grade your staff. Who would you rehire, and who wouldn't you rehire? Examine why you wouldn't rehire certain people.

- Get feedback from your staff to find out what they think of you, your managers and your company.

- Work on your communications throughout the company – communication is key to everyone pulling in the same direction.

- Aim for short, time-bound meetings with a clear agenda to keep everyone engaged.

- Use feedback from employees and customers to come up with monthly themes to keep everyone excited.

The meetings you have cement how you communicate with all your current staff. Now let's look outside the company. The core of the business is recruiting well.

8
Recruit Well

Hopefully you are already experiencing some changes within your company. And hopefully any new people you recruit will get the culture – that tends to be why the best people choose to work for a business, so you need to make sure you set your culture out clearly right from the beginning.

The first rule of recruitment is to have a solid written process that can be followed by anyone to hire the right people – those who believe in the company. There are six main parts to a recruitment process, but all too often elements are skipped in certain areas. I find that this process works for most companies, whether you are looking for skilled or unskilled labour.

Who and what do you want?

The place to start is to break down who and what you need. It would be no surprise if I said everyone was different, or if I said anyone can be taught to do a particular task or role; however, not everyone can do it well and with ease. Different people have different personality traits. Some people are outgoing, others reserved and introverted. Some are task orientated and love detail but others are people orientated and more creative.

Many people make the mistake of recruiting more of the same, whether they are replacing someone who has left or expanding a department. This can work, but there are a couple of tricks you can try:

- If you have, say, twenty production staff, picture the ideal person for the role. Maybe one of your team excels over all others, or maybe a combination of your current team members' talents in one person would make them the ideal recruit.

- Make sure the flow of the process is streamlined enough so you recruit the right person for the role. Or is the role open ended, in which case you may need a mix of profiles? (We will discuss profiling in the next chapter.)

Once you decide on the ideal candidate, write a job advert or description that will appeal to the right profile. Use words and headlines that will make it jump out at that person. The right job advert is just as important as the right sales advert – they both have to appeal to who you want, not just everyone.

How do you get that person?

There are three main ways:

- Recommendation (ask your team and people within your circle)

- Advertise and hope the right people apply

- Enlist the services of a recruitment agent or headhunter

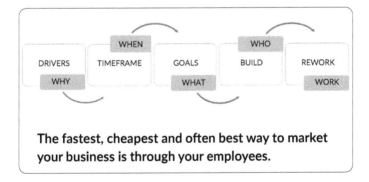

The fastest, cheapest and often best way to market your business is through your employees.

The route you choose depends on the skills and experience required for the role. If you are recruiting for a management or specialised post, then I would suggest the headhunter route. They will know the field and be able to find the right people, saving you a lot of time. Generally headhunters will not charge anything until you pick one of their candidates, so let them do the hard work.

Make sure the job advert includes clear instructions. You need to see if candidates can follow orders, eg apply with curriculum vitae (CV) and covering letter. Also make sure they supply a reference number. This is really important as you can then set up an auto-response stating when you will look at the applicants and move the email into the correct folder.

If you are advertising a part-time or low-skilled role, generally using a job board, social media or one of the thousands of recruitment websites will be fine. With this method, it is important to narrow the type of advert you use, ie be specific. If you need experience in something, make sure you state what experience you require. You can burn a lot of time trying to get thousands of applicants; remember, you only need to find the right one, so if five apply and one is the star, that saves a lot of time.

The next stage is to go through the CVs and decide on what you are looking for. Work out a top ten (this, of course, depends on the number of applicants you get and the number of roles you are recruiting for). Have an email template created for the unsuccessful candidates, which saves loads of time as you don't have to write responses individually, but make it personable. Nothing is worse for an unsuccessful candidate than receiving a robotic email telling them they didn't get the job.

Once you have selected the best people, the next stage is the interview process.

Interviews

I recommend a telephone interview to start with, as this will quickly separate the wheat from the chaff. It also stops any unconscious bias based on appearances. This may sound funny, but we are all human, and we all make visual judgements.

You can have interview templates that you use for specific roles, depending on where you are getting the applicants from. It is important the questions are relevant. You wouldn't ask a technical person the same questions as a salesperson.

Telephone interviews should flow like any conversation. There is nothing worse than confusing a good applicant because you're asking them a question that has no relevance to the role. I also recommend you write the questions in plain English, and then allow the interviewer to ask them in their own way.

There are a few standard telephone interview questions to ask, but what you really want to know is whether the candidate has a passion for the role:

- What is your favourite part of [role-specific task]?

- What is your motivation for wanting to join our team?

- What do you like most about your current role?

- What do you like least about your current role?

- What experience do you have with [role-specific task or software]?

- Why are you looking to leave your current position?

- What can you bring to this role over other applicants?

- What would you like to be doing in 3–5 years?

- Which of our values most resonates with you and why?

- If I were to hire you for this job and I granted you three promises with regards to working here, what would they be?

- Do you have any questions for us?

A few tips are:

- Keep questions specific to the role.

- Make sure you know how the candidate found you, eg a job advert or recruiter.

- Understand their motives. Ask things like, 'What advice would you give your previous boss? And why?'

- Ask them to give examples of the work they have done.

- Ask what motivates them.

- Find out their outside interests. Do they have hobbies etc?

- Importantly, do you feel aligned with them? This saves a lot of wasted time in the future.

You can visit my website for some templated interview questions that you can download for the different types of role: gilescleverley.com

Always pre-book the telephone interviews with the applicants and make sure you leave at least a twenty-minute gap between each. Usually these types of interview take five to ten minutes, depending on the detail required for the position.

You are mainly trying to find out if the person can (a) do the job and (b) fit the culture of the business. Never forget how important culture is. You can train a person to improve their skills, but you can rarely change their beliefs and values.

Then you move on to the face-to-face interview. This is an exciting time if you have completed the telephone interviews properly, because you should be set up for finding the right person. But this stage can be a long, laborious process if you skip the telephone interview stage.

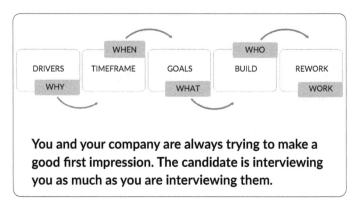

You and your company are always trying to make a good first impression. The candidate is interviewing you as much as you are interviewing them.

There are two ways of interviewing face to face: one at a time or in groups. For 90% of roles, I prefer the group interview process. The dynamic in the room tends to pull the cream to the top. The 10% is generally for a senior management position. These candidates should have a certain pedigree and experience, which means you will be able to see if they fit the culture and beliefs of the business without the need to put them in a group interview environment. If the type of job you need filled is quite niche and specialist, you may just go straight for a one-to-one interview too.

I favour day-long one-to-one interviews when you need to test the applicant's skill level, for example, software technicians. Let them meet different team members and see if they are a fit for your culture.

The key to any successful group interview is firstly to ask the candidates if they are happy with a group interview when you invite them in. No one ever objects if they really want the job, and they will then be prepared. If you do not pre-warn them, they may feel uncomfortable right from the beginning.

I would suggest you either email the candidates before the group interview or give them a printout that they can read before you begin, telling them:

- Your company's core values/ethos

- Your company's golden rules/rules of the game

- The detailed job description

You need to know if they buy in to and get the values of the business and understand the job exactly. Don't waste time going through the group interview answering basic questions that the printout can already have answered.

Generally, a group interview will take no longer than one hour. I would suggest the maximum is ten attendees, and six to eight is optimum. Any more than ten and you will run out of time.

There are lots of different ways of holding group interviews. Some people prefer to hire a room in a hotel or conference centre, but I would generally suggest you hold them at the business premises they will be working in. This will give them a better feel for the place, but if you do not have the facilities for this, hiring a room somewhere is fine.

It is always best to come up with your own questions that are centred on your business and culture, but I would suggest starting with people introducing themselves, and ending with questions and answers people may have.

It's all about trying to get to know the real person, not the person on their best behaviour. I recommend having two people present at the interview and making sure both interviewers are introduced, but only one runs the interview. It can be difficult and add tension if two interviewers are crossing over each other.

Once the interview is complete, give the candidates a clear timeframe for future communication, for example, 'We will be deciding by X date.' As soon as the candidates have left, both interviewers write on a separate piece of paper their first and second choice, and then reveal the answers. This is powerful stuff, as surprisingly, 80% of the time both interviewers will pick the same people.

Have you chosen the right one?

Before you make the job offer to your favourite candidate, always do these two things:

- Get them to complete an online profile (numerous available)

- Get two references

Over 60% of companies do not follow up references, but this is important. How you contact them is your decision, but I generally prefer to phone referees with a list of about six questions. When you speak to them, you can feel the person's emotions towards the candidate. If you send an email or letter asking for a written reference, the referee is likely only to write the positive things as they may be fearful of repercussions.

Some questions you might ask are:

- What was the candidate's length of service? You may be surprised how many candidates cover up how many jobs they have had.

- What were the key tasks they were responsible for? Some people say they were managing others when they were not.

- Was the notice period worked?

- Would the referee rehire the candidate?

- What few words would they use to describe the person?

There are lots of questions you could ask, it really does depend on the role, but always take up references.

Also, make sure you run the candidate's profile, and trust the profiling. If their profile is not naturally suited to the role, they will always struggle completing the tasks as they will not be performing to their strengths. If your number-one candidate is far from the ideal profile, this can be your chance to profile the second or third choice from the group interviews. So many people make the mistake of recruiting the person they like the most, when the main thing is that the recruit fits the overall culture of the business and their profile suits the role you need filling.

The next stage is to make the job offer. Remember, this is the start of that person's relationship with the business, so make everything as clear as possible from the outset. If you will give them a three-month trial, then tell them this in the offer letter. It is always best to be completely upfront.

Overcome as many potential fears and insecurities as possible in the job offer. Have a structured letter that explains:

- Where to go to start
- Who to meet
- Best time to arrive (I find a short first day can help ease a new recruit in)
- Uniform/dress code

- Whether they need security passes and where to collect them if they do

- Whether they need identification, and if so, tell them what to bring

- Parking – where is best and whether they need a permit

Give them as many handy tips as possible. Answering potential questions now will save time in the future. If you are unsure what to include, ask the people around you who have recently been employed by the business. What did they fear on their first day? What information would have been nice? How about a welcoming bunch of flowers?

Day one

The induction process can be where a lot of companies fail as they don't appreciate how this affects the way the new recruit and the team will work together. I have made all the mistakes that can be made, from letting people loose on customers without training to not explaining the production side of things properly, so I know what I'm talking about here.

For a company to be successful and grow solidly, it must treat a recruit's induction as hugely important (with ongoing training and support a close second). You are hoping the person you have recruited (always treat them as individuals, even if you are recruiting fifty at a time) is going to be exactly what you want them to be, and will be everything they said they were in the interview. If you have done your job well, they will be as near to that as makes no difference, and all you need to do is shape and mould them to be the person you were hoping for. How fast this happens depends on how you treat them in their first week.

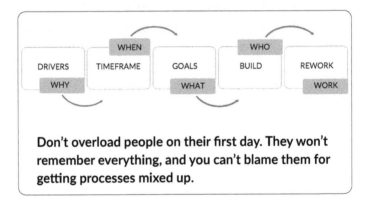

Don't overload people on their first day. They won't remember everything, and you can't blame them for getting processes mixed up.

Remember to celebrate every recruit's start. More companies celebrate when people leave than when they join.

What exactly do people want from an induction? They want to be given the guided tour and told how to perform and what is expected of them. This really comes back to the rules of the game that we discussed in Chapter 6, but it goes beyond that. The rules are great for giving people boundaries, but what the induction should do is give people a real feel for the company and explain things in layman's terms. And you must have a detailed employee manual specifically for new recruits.

What should go into the starter's manual?

- An overview of the company – keep it real and remember you are a people-centric business
- The basics – locations/hours of business etc
- Dress codes, when breaks can be taken and where the toilets are
- Acceptable behaviours such as tidiness and cleanliness, and the attitude you expect
- Health and safety, fire training and who the first aiders are
- The benefits your company brings to the new employee
- How holidays and sickness work
- Golden rules, values, beliefs etc
- How to treat people – customers/colleagues/suppliers
- Basics such as answering the phone with a smile and helping others
- How to use a main database (although this usually needs a separate manual)
- Security issues

- Frugal behaviour

- Structure of the business

- Disciplinary procedures

- Appraisals

- Courses and training availability

- Awards and incentives

- Events

- Social activities

It is worth spending time on the starter's manual as this is the first thing people will read and remember. You have a limited amount of time to forge good habits and routines with new starters.

There are lots of other steps to take on the recruit's first day, like filling in forms, taking emergency contact information, etc. I don't want to go through this here, but I would suggest you create a detailed first-day process that can be improved over time with continual feedback.

Employee bio

The recruit's first day is often the start of how they mean to go on, and creating an employee bio can really get them enthusiastic about working with you.

You want to know what sort of person they are on the inside as well as outside. What are their goals (personal and career)? What makes them tick? What funny stories do they have to tell? Is there any family stuff they want to share? If you take the time to get to know your team, it will always increase your staff retention. And all these things are important and worth knowing.

Helping your employees achieve their goals can be a true team effort, and is far better than shutting them in a room all day until they reach retirement age, and then giving them a gold watch. Help them excel, fire their passion, give them a reason for belonging to *your* business, not just any old business.

The world is getting faster in all areas, including people's attention span. They will jump from one website to another if they do not find what they're looking for within ten seconds, and may do similar with employment. Fifty years ago, people looked at getting a job for life; now people will jump from company to company relatively fearlessly in the western world. How are you going to keep your people enthused so they feel like they belong with your business?

The employee bio is hopefully the first step to convincing them that they are now working for a company that cares, showing them that you walk the talk. And when it comes around to the next appraisal, the bio gives you a benchmark to work from.

Everything that you do within your business should always have the end goal of making your employees proud to wear the badge. If your business card does not land with a boom, you have so much more work to do. The key is to keep asking the golden questions:

- How can we improve?

- What can we do better?

In his book *Break Through*,[10] David Carter talks about getting people to find their North Star. If you can find what your people's North Star is – the goal that really lights their fire – and help them to follow it, you will get massive results.

At this point, I would like to bring you back to remembering your goal. You have to truly want each person to be able to complete a task or process better than you ever could. If a person is not really interested in staying with your business, you cannot make them love their job, but you can provide a great environment, a raison d'être. If they still do not want to be in the role, then this is their choice.

What is the key to creating a great working environment for your recruits? Great leaders inspire their people to think together and act together to make a difference by:

---

10   D C M Carter, *Break Through: Learn the secrets of the world's leading mentor and become the best you can be* (Piatkus, 2012)

- Creating a compelling vision beyond the numbers

- Inspiring others to stretch beyond their perceived limits

Do this right from the start with your recruits.

Culture vultures

Remember the best ideas will usually come from within your organisation. But people will only speak out if they feel wanted and appreciated.

There will always be people in business who don't feel they have to adhere to the rules or follow all the procedures. These people can often cause issues and drain the life out of all the people around them.

You need to have zero tolerance with this. If people within the business see someone getting away with slacking or not behaving in a fitting manner, it won't take long for others to feel it is OK to behave in the same manner. The best way of dealing with culture vultures is to probe into why they are behaving in this way, but make it clear that eventually, they will have to shape up or jump ship.

The vultures are usually a particular problem when you start adjusting your company's culture. You cannot create a culture within five minutes and expect it to last when you are no longer working every day within the business. Be sure you have people who love what they do and live the company culture so they can carry it on.

Remember the golden question: 'Would you recommend working for this company to your best friends and family?'

Key takeaways

You always want to recruit the right talent to join your teams. Remember that the best people join a company because of its culture more than anything else, so make sure your culture is clear and lived by everyone associated with your business.

I recommend a six-step process when you're looking to recruit new team members:

- Work out exactly who and what you want.

- How will you get that person? Decide how you will advertise the position, check the CVs that come in and make a shortlist for interview.

- Interview your favourite candidates, first over the phone and then face to face. The face-to-face interviews can be done singularly or in groups of up to ten.

- When you have chosen your favourite candidate from the interviews, speak to two referees and profile the candidate to make sure they fit the role.

- On your new recruit's first day, make sure they feel from the outset that they belong with your company. Celebrate their arrival.

- Create an employee bio for your recruit, really getting to know them well.

Finally, watch out for the culture vultures among your employees who will look to destroy your team as fast as you build it up.

Let's now have a look at profiling to ensure every hire is the best fit for your company.

9
Profiling

Until I really understood the value of what profiling can do and the 'untainted' information it provides, I thought it was just a load of psychological mumbo jumbo. But actually, it is the key to understanding your team, the people around you, and why they do what they do. It also explains why certain things that others do annoy you, and with this understanding, the annoyance can disappear overnight. It becomes clearer whether they are doing things according to their favoured approach, or just being lazy or disruptive.

What is profiling? There are multiple types of personalities; this is how people are hardwired. The problem is that most people don't understand why others do what they do and like what they like. For example,

I couldn't think of anything worse than reading through a 300-page safety assessment, but for some people, the more detail, the better.

You might now be saying, 'What has this got to do with me, Giles?' The straight answer is, 'A lot.' I can guarantee that once you understand what people's profiles are, you will know what makes them tick. And this ticking is in every way: the jobs/tasks they will enjoy; the best way to give them praise; the type of working environment they like; and the profiles and personalities of the people they will naturally work well with.

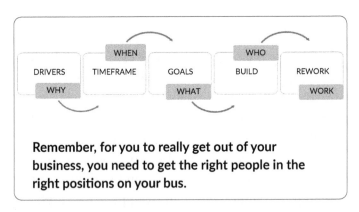

Remember, for you to really get out of your business, you need to get the right people in the right positions on your bus.

If you have a team conflict, with profiling, you can take away the personal element from people's actions and explain it through their profiles. For example, if someone is annoyed with someone else due to their untidiness or lack of detail, you can attack the issues from a different angle and use profiling to put measures in place to stop it happening again and help the flow of work. It's like saying, 'I may not like the actions you performed, but I still like you as a person.'

To get the optimum from people, you first need to understand what roles they will naturally enjoy doing. Then you will get the most from them with the least resistance.

DISC profiling

What exactly is profiling? There are lots of variations, but here are a few that I have tried:

- DISC profiling
- Talent Dynamics
- Six Hats
- Devine Profiling
- Myers Briggs

All have their pros and cons, so do some research to find out which works best for your business. Personally, I like DISC due to its simplistic methodology.

The other thing I like about DISC is that it breaks down personality types into four. DISC stands for:

- D = Dominance
- I = Influence
- S = Steadiness
- C = Conscientiousness

DISC was once described to me as different types of birds, then it just clicked. Wow – how easy to understand. Just imagine the personality/behaviours of these birds:

- The dominant eagle, going straight for the kill
- The influential parrot, talkative and persuasive
- The steady dove, nurturing those around them
- The conscientious owl, thoughtful and intelligent

Most people usually have one dominant trait, one or two middle traits, and one will be minimal. People's dominant profile can switch when they're under pressure. For example, a person might be either quieter than normal or much more direct.

Using DISC with selling

Profiling is great for your team, but if you can learn to use it whenever you meet people, it comes into great effect in a sales environment. Generally people's homes and offices will reflect their profile, so let's looks at some examples of what to look out for:

- D = pictures of large fish caught or sporting achievements, all action stuff. Maybe awards displayed prominently (the peacock approach).

- I = generally a bit messy. Pictures of group events: parties, weddings, barbecues they have attended. It's all about popularity for I personalities.

- S = these people may have a couple of pictures of family and homely items scattered around.

- C = usually very little, as C personalities like to be tidy and organised. They may possibly have one picture of close family.

How can profiling help your business?

First of all, remember to profile yourself to understand what makes you tick. You will then truly understand how you feel about profiling.

It's funny how people react to profiling. Usually they're reluctant at first, then once they complete the test and their profile is produced, they're quite upbeat and agree with most points. Remember, we're all different. For example, I would hate having to do an in-depth task, but would be fine speaking in front of 500 people. Someone who is mainly C/S would love the detail and hate speaking to more than ten people.

How exactly can profiling help your business? I would start by profiling your teams – senior and mid-level managers at least. You can then merge these to create a collective profile that shows how weighted the teams and your business are towards the different profiles. For example, a firm of accountants would probably lean heavily towards a C (detail-orientated) profile, whereas a team of nurses would be leaning towards an S (caring and nurturing). Doctors would be more a combination of S and D (dominant).

How do you bring profiling into a company? You must guard against mass scepticism, so remember your goal is to share the results. You also have to get people's permission (don't worry, they're all likely to give it).

Then you follow a series of steps:

- **Step one:** explain profiling in brief to all the people you want profile.

- **Step two:** get them to complete the profiles (most are online surveys). Ask people to complete the profile in a normal (non-stressed) environment as the results may slightly skew if they feel under pressure.

- **Step three:** sit down with each person individually and discuss their profile. This is the biggest eye opener – it never fails to amaze me how much people agree with the results, and they are often just as surprised how accurate profiling is.

- **Step four:** gather people together (I prefer groups of five or six) and let everyone read through each other's profiles. This is normally fun, but make sure you are controlling the conversation and keeping it positive.

Profiling should clear a lot of misunderstandings that people have and explain why they do what they do in the way they do it. It isn't to annoy others; it's just their way.

When I first started profiling, I thought one team member, who I'd always liked and respected, was relatively carefree and not particularly detail orientated, but when we completed the profiles, it showed that he was actually a C. As a result, I asked him to create the company manuals and his face lit up. He did an amazing job, far better than I could ever have imagined, but before the profiling, I would never have picked him for the task.

Recruitment with profiling

Profiling has made a huge difference to how my businesses recruit people. It gives the answers and understanding that you cannot get from anyone in an interview, or even a trial period.

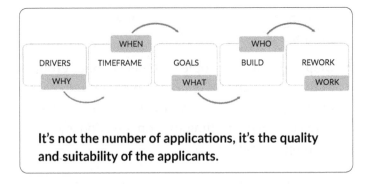

It's not the number of applications, it's the quality and suitability of the applicants.

Again, there are four steps to follow:

- **Step one:** the initial stage is looking at the job description and generating an ideal profile from the tasks you want the recruit to complete.

- **Step two:** now you know the type of person you want, write the job advert to appeal to them using key words and phrases that resonate with their profile. If you want a carer/nurse, write about comfort, helping people etc. A sales role aimed at a D profile would need to be firmer with results-driven, challenging language.

- **Step three:** you should only get people who are drawn by the wording that appeals to the right profile applying, the main advantage being that you will get a lot fewer people who are wrong for the job. This is a great money- and time-saving tip.

- **Step four:** during the telephone interview, you can ask candidates questions around the job advert or description. The answers will indicate their profile and you will get a clear differentiator for choosing the right applicant for the role you need filled.

People who are not naturally suited to a role will fight against it, whether mentally or physically. They may well stick at it and adjust when they are in the role, but they will never get in true flow. Have you ever met people who seem to complete certain tasks with ease? Or people who act differently when they're in and out of work? These are clear indicators of whether someone is in flow, or not.

The most powerful way to adjust to the person/people you are engaging with is to understand yourself. Once you crack this understanding, you will find you have a lot more patience with the opposites of your profile. And the first step is realising that there is no superior or inferior profile; there are just profiles that suit certain tasks and roles better than others.

Now that you can use profiling to know and understand the people within your business, it's time to break down what tasks have to be done in-house and what can be outsourced. The knock-on effects of getting this wrong can ruin a company's reputation.

Outsource or insource

Your ultimate aim is to take yourself out of the business. All things need to be done, just not by you. Don't sweat the small stuff; create a process and get someone else to ensure it is followed.

Before you can get to this point, you need to know each individual process that has to be completed for the business to run, then look at the potential impacts of outsourcing. The biggest mistake companies make is only looking at the bottom line, but cost is often the last place you should look once the other factors have been thrashed out.

For each process, ask:

- What would be the impact on the end user if the process was outsourced?

- Can it be outsourced with a minimum impact on the business and its customers?

- Why do you want it outsourced?

- Is there any underlying value in doing it in-house?

Generally, these four questions are all you need to get a good feel for whether you are making the right decision to outsource.

What is outsourcing? In a nutshell, it is getting an external individual or company to perform anything that you may currently do in-house. Outsourcing can be to a local, national or international company or individual.

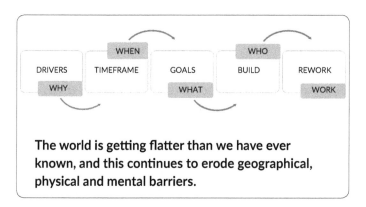

The world is getting flatter than we have ever known, and this continues to erode geographical, physical and mental barriers.

The most obvious outsourcing over the past ten years has been call centres/customer service, but there are lots of other outsourcing options. Pretty much any of your departments could potentially be outsourced, but you do need to think carefully about this. You are entrusting an operational aspect of the business to a third party, so you must be clear and understand the implications if the third party fails or doesn't have the same standards as you. You can't guarantee someone else will train their team as well as you do and have the same beliefs and values as you. To outsource effectively, you will have to assess your business's weaknesses, pass those tasks over and concentrate on your goals.

The high art with outsourcing is getting someone or another company to do a task better than you could, hopefully at the same if not a reduced cost. You need to research this and really get down to the numbers. Outsourcing companies charge for the volume of work they take on, so you need to ask yourself, 'If the business grows and we put more work through the external company, will it remain economical?'

In my experience, these are the most popular departments to outsource (mainly through installing the right technology):

- Accounts – this can be done either in the same country or abroad. Many firms in India, for example, will specialise in the tax laws of certain countries, so make sure you choose the right one for your business.

- Legal – this is similar to the accounts inasmuch as the laws vary from country to country. Lots of due diligence is imperative.

- Customer relations – call answering and handling complaints.

- Installations and contractors.

- Websites and marketing.

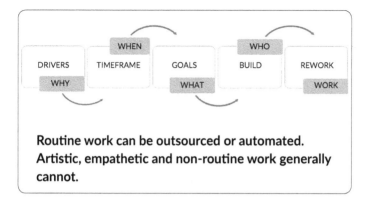

Routine work can be outsourced or automated. Artistic, empathetic and non-routine work generally cannot.

The main advantage of using a specialist firm is that the staff will be highly trained in their area of expertise and should be able to add much more breadth of knowledge. Also, the right company will have invested in the services they provide.

An example of this is a postal service. You as a business might send 200 letters per month, which probably means you pay someone to print, pack and post the letters, and the postage will probably be the retail cost. A specialist mailing company will have the machines to auto-print, pack and frank the letters. They will also get better rates for postage as they bulk send/ deliver. If you can find the right tipping point, it will be more economical to outsource this than complete the role in-house.

SIDE NOTE – TIPPING POINT

All tasks that are regularly completed within your company will have a tipping point, so you need to calculate this. Many companies will charge a retainer/set-up fee or minimum amount, so taking letters as an example, it might not be economical unless you send 500+ per month. If you are planning on switching to email communications in the future, it wouldn't be advisable to commit to any lengthy postal contract.

I don't understand why large corporates put so little value on the customer experience. It is much cheaper to keep an existing customer than attract new ones, so think hard about how any outsourcing affects the end user. The customer must be key. This needs to be thrashed out – if they won't like it, why?

For example, many people have a dislike of foreign call centres. It angers and frustrates customers when they can barely understand or be understood by the person they're speaking to, so look at native-tongue call centres.

Websites and information technology (IT) are perfect to outsource to a specialist company. It can be an absolute minefield trying to keep up with the various algorithms. It is nice to have an in-house IT department as generally you get an immediate response, but often internal people get complacent and may not always be striving for the best practices. As people naturally keep busy with the day-to-day tasks, the constant push and willingness to stay up to date can decline over time.

A lot of the questions and scenarios around outsourcing are dependent on the type of business you are in. If you run a construction company, then you want the phone answered, but usually a call back within a stated period will suffice. A hospital emergency ward, on the other hand, will need the phones manned 24 hours a day, 365 days a year.

If you are unsure, I would recommend looking at the best in your industry. What do they do? Why do you think they are the best? Remember, do not confuse the biggest with the best; it's reputation that counts. Look at who you like. For example, if you particularly like contacting a certain supplier, find out if they outsource the service you use.

One big advantage of outsourcing to the right company is that you are the client. So as long as you keep a close eye on the role the company plays and mystery shop occasionally, you can usually be confident that part of the business is running well. Remember, if it is not, you can always move to another company to outsource the service to. This can be a major step in getting you out of the business.

Key takeaways

Profiling is key to understanding your team. In this chapter, we looked at:

- What profiling is – knowing how people are hardwired and why they do what they do

- How profiling can help you make sure the right people are in the right positions for them

- The four DISC personalities: dominant, influential, steady and conscientious

- How to use profiling outside of your team

- The four steps of profiling and what to do when you have the results

- How profiling can help you write a job advertisement to appeal to the right personalities for the role

With the understanding that profiling can bring, you are now in a strong position to decide what tasks need to stay in-house and which you can outsource, moving you one step closer to freedom from your business.

Now let's looks at the final W of getting you out of the business: work. This is when the fun really begins!

PART FIVE
WORK

Keep moving forward.

10
Momentum

Momentum for me is what most executive teams and company owners fail to focus on. Most companies are OK with setting goals, but they usually set them only once a year. The goals are not detailed and the business owners and managers don't shout about them enough. There is almost a mentality that they should be secret. They shouldn't!

The brain is a magnificent tool that has a great way of discarding things it doesn't think you need to know anymore. For example, have you ever smelled something for a minute, and then the smell just seems to go away? It doesn't really. The smelly dog, for example, is still there; it's just that your brain has eliminated its odour from the relevant present.

Pretty much all company leaders I speak to say, 'If I'm not pushing the team, no one else will.' This is where you need to make sure you are leading and inspiring others, then they will drive forward as one. American entrepreneur Jim Rohn used the 80–20 rule for this – spend 80% of your time with the 20% of people who need the most help.

Before you generate momentum through others, you need to start with you first – self-motivation.

Self-motivation

Understand why you want your goals – in the context of this book, they're the ones that will ultimately lead to you freeing yourself from your business. Get clear in your own head – what will freedom mean to you and your personal life? You must get excited to drive forwards, otherwise it will be a slow meander. Get focused and into action.

YouTube can be good if you need a little inspiration, a shot of adrenalin. Just type in 'motivation' or 'inspiring story' and find thousands of video clips. Wrap your internal motivation around the goals on your dream board, BHAG, bucket list. In Chapter 2, we spoke about affirmations, which can be a powerful ally to help you get through to the team.

Depending on how long you have been in the business and your overall profile, affirmations might be completely out of your comfort zone. I wouldn't recommend trying to be someone you are not, as your integrity must remain intact. You also do not have to be a great public speaker to get your team following you; getting someone to work with you might be the biggest breakthrough.

Bill Gates, for example, built a powerful business without jumping up on tables and shouting inspiration, but he did know his why. The same goes for Steve Jobs of Apple, who was really good at portraying his vision so the teams around him could go and create it. Both Gates and Jobs started with themselves, their own why, and grew it to inspire others.

Team momentum

When you're clear on your why and you have self-motivation behind it, you need to transfer your momentum to the team. Get them to own the vision and want to achieve more.

The hardest time can be the beginning of the process. If you are looking at changing the direction of the business so you can free yourself from it, then you need to adjust where it is pointing. A good analogy is a large boat. Try to change direction when it is not moving fast, and the wheel just doesn't want to turn easily; so the rate at which the boat turns is non-existent to begin with. Then slowly, it starts to move round. You need to limber up the business and get it moving faster and more freely. So when you alter its trajectory, you can easily get it heading in the right direction.

Teams grow more quickly together. A company that is truly in flow can be a beautiful thing. How many teams in your business are pulling in different directions? Are any pulling against change? Find out why.

For a business to take on its own momentum, you need to make sure the right people are on your boat. Rather than people who turn up every day purely to pick up a pay cheque, you need people who really get the culture of the business and want to help it succeed.

The first thing you need to do towards creating the right culture is to make sure you open the lines of communication. Has everyone within your business got access to you? I'm not saying that if you employ 10,000 people, they can all call you about mundane things, but you must be there and accessible. Do you communicate with your teams? The great inventions of emails and intranet sites mean you can communicate much more easily and cheaply than ever before.

If you have marketing departments that can generate newsletters, video clips etc, make use of this resource, but often it is the personal touch that speaks volumes.

A four- to five-line email can break down barriers. Most employees think that the MD of a company just drinks Moët and nibbles caviar all day, so give them a piece of you, which is all they will want. Your ultimate goal is to make sure the people who will be running the business when you have gone are open with communication as well. If you're open, then over time, the management levels will also be open; it really is that simple.

Then look at how the departments communicate internally and externally. I am a great believer in internal meetings, but they need to be focused with a clear agenda, script and timeframe. These are my top eight things that must happen at a meeting:

- Structure – have a template for all meetings.

- Time – daily meetings must be a maximum of twenty minutes. Be strict.

- Always be aware that some big issues may come up, so arrange a time to address these after the meeting.

- Stand up and be counted – everyone should be involved and present. Do not let people wander off or, if the meeting is under twenty minutes, sit down.

- Daily meetings are a great time for revisiting visions/goals etc. There are always subtle ways of maintaining momentum.

- Make sure meetings not only cover the tasks for the day and/or week, but also include praise, eg if someone went beyond the normal call of duty for a client or stayed late to complete an urgent task. Thank the team member – remember, often acknowledgement is all people want.

- Issues. This is vital. If a team member has a personal issue, they can bring down the atmosphere in the whole department. If they bring their issues to the team, they will get support and the team will join together and help, rather than moan about the individual behind their back. A zero triangulation rule can be a great way for quashing aimless tittle-tattle.

- Team members rotate who runs the meetings, giving real drive. Then it's not just the manager hiding behind their clipboard and asserting their authority.

I remember I had a chap working with me who was happy to start at any hour of the morning and was always generous with his time at work, but as soon as the clock hit 5pm, he was out of the door. He also never went for drinks after work or joined in with any social events. It wasn't until we were able to address this issue honestly that he explained his personal circumstances, and then everyone understood. Transparency makes for a much better working environment.

Company culture and recruitment

When you interview candidates, crucial questions to ask are: 'Do you want to work for a company like this? Do you align with our culture?'

Don't be a company that appeals to everyone. This is the mistake that many businesses make when they're looking for their ideal targets, both recruits and customers. You want A-grade people working for you and buying from you.

The nice thing with showing people who you are as a business is that you can be clear with them from the start. There's zero mutual mystification. Do you like us, do we like you?

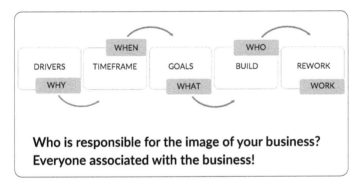

Who is responsible for the image of your business? Everyone associated with the business!

The funniest thing I hear people say is, 'It's business, not personal.' What a load of rubbish – business *is* personal. You don't buy from a brick wall, you buy from the person selling and working in a business. If you recruit a horrible person, that person will make customers think your business flows in the same vein.

An interview is similar to a first date – for various people it is either easier or harder, but the human aspect is the same. If people are too boastful, you may not like them; if they are too quiet, you may not like them; if they do not align with your beliefs, you certainly won't like them. Unfortunately, most companies look at this from the wrong perspective. They are always thinking about whether they like the applicant. But what if the candidate doesn't like you?

This is an important factor to consider. If someone wants to work for your business because they just get it and align with your culture, they will:

- Work harder
- Work for less money (I'm not saying pay low wages, but reasonable will suffice)
- Not clock watch
- Suit and fit the team
- Attract more A-grade clients

There are three levels within the recruitment process that you need to follow in this order to find the person who really aligns with your company culture:

1. Find the profile that best fits the culture of the organisation (job descriptions and adverts are key to this).

2. Profile the applicants to make sure they suit the role you want filled.

3. Assess if they have the skills or experience you require (it is last on the list as most things can be trained).

If you are in a specialist industry or the position requires the candidates to have specific skills and qualifications, make sure you clarify this in your job description and advert. Remember, if they don't have the minimum requirements for the job, they shouldn't be sitting in front of you. This is wasting time, and what is my number-one hate? Wasting time!

Company culture and the team

When you have people who fit the company culture on your team, you must be walking the talk. You need to make sure, from the ground upwards, that everyone gets what your business is about as a whole. But how do you get the team on board and pulling forward?

The best place to start is on a one-to-one basis at the time of your yearly, bi-yearly or quarterly reviews.

This gives an open environment for questions and cynicism to be answered head on.

Do you currently have team and staff reviews? Do people look forward to them or moan about them? Often, people think they're going to be told the same old rubbish at their review, then hopefully get an inflation-based pay rise, but this is way off the mark. Reviews should be the time when people feel free to express exactly what they think and feel about the company, and plan their careers with your business. Where do they want to be? How do they think their performance is going and why?

In advance of a review, send a feedback form to each team member, covering anything that will be relevant to give structure to the review. Give them one to two weeks to complete the form and send it to the person who will carry out the review. It is important that the person doing the review is the team member's immediate manager, not the overall manager. This further cements the relationship.

There also needs to be a form for the appraiser to complete to score the team member. It is important they do this without bias, and without reading the scores the person has given themselves.

Then it's time for the review. This should be scheduled for at least one hour. The appraiser and team member go through all the answers and the scores, then discuss everything. It is important to be open and honest; if either side isn't, then there will be less potential for growth and improving the work environment. You need to really understand why the person does what they do and if they enjoy it. Are they slacking because they're bored, or is there just not enough work to do?

The last part of the review is to go through some of the plans and goals the organisation has. Where is it heading? Discuss if the staff member might be able to go for any new positions (this is especially useful for companies opening new branches or expanding into new markets). You will soon find out if they are on your bus fully or just picking up their pay cheque every month.

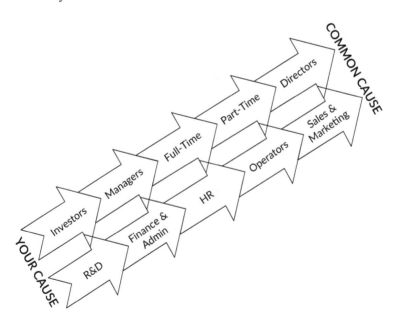

Remember, the main reason for the review is not to tell the staff member what and how to behave, but to understand why they do what they do. Then you can really explain the rules of the game and they can decide if they want to stay on board or if they feel your bus is going in the wrong direction for them.

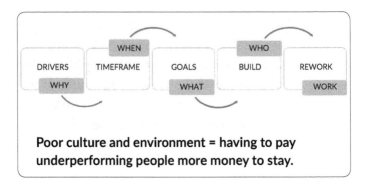

Poor culture and environment = having to pay underperforming people more money to stay.

In my experience, people will usually shape up and get on board with how you want the company to act and feel, or they will leave. A person leaving can feel painful at the time, but if they don't align with the culture, you will always need to pay them more to stay motivated and stick around. Some people love working for a corporate, being a small cog in a huge machine. Others prefer to work for a small team and be an important cog. Both are right – it depends on the individual.

A good part of the review is the action going forward – the no mutual mystification part. If I as a team leader know what drives a person and what I can do to help them, I will do my best to do this. If I as a team member want to grow within the business I work for, I want to feel like my manager gets me. It is imperative that you decide on actions moving forward (the assessor can set calendar reminders for follow-ups etc).

When you or your managers complete reviews, it is important that you send a copy of everything you have discussed and agreed to the team member so you both know where you're heading. You can then use this report to make sure issues have been sorted and monitor how motivated the team member is. If the situation has got worse, why?

Team building

I cannot emphasise enough how important team-building exercises are. They are a huge part of ensuring individuals go out of their way to help each other. They also allow the managers to become 'one of the guys/girls' instead of being just the boss. Remember, if you like people on a one-to-one basis, working with them is always more enjoyable. Team building is a huge part of the process of getting the company in flow.

Give the role of organising team-building events to someone who:

- Understands why you're having the event

- Manages the budget

- Makes sure the event has structure and is fun/ relaxed

It is important to ask the team members what they like to do. If they just want to have a few drinks and shoot the breeze, that's fine. Sometimes team events like go karting can be good. As long as the focus is away from work and all about the activity.

Another good team-building activity is volunteering for charity or local causes. This has a double impact: it is great for team morale and good for the profile of the company, a win-win.

All people need to be rewarded. This is human nature. Some people like to have their egos massaged by everyone knowing they are the best employees, others would prefer it to be a private thank you, but what remains the same is that all people like to be acknowledged for their efforts. In numerous employee surveys, this comes either top or high up on the list.

In one of my businesses, Syn-Star, we award an 'Above and Beyond' trophy each month to whoever the team members think has done the most for customers that month. It might be that someone gave extra help to a customer or stayed on late to fix an issue. Whatever it is, each team member can send in nominations, then the winner gets their lunch bought for them every Friday of the following month as a thank you.

Rewards and trophies can be for individuals/departments or different locations. The main thing is to come up with something the team can get involved with and behind, which why my business's trophy is awarded by the team. Get your team behind the rewards and get them excited.

SIDE NOTE - IT'S NOT ABOUT THE BENJAMINS

Most people say they are motivated by money, but they're not. It is just the easy answer. People only look for a new job if they don't get their current role (if they don't truly understand why they are doing the job or the company they are doing it for).

You do need to pay a fair wage, but you don't have to pay the most in your industry.

Nurture momentum

A man can throw seeds on the ground, come back six months later and some crops will have grown through natural rain and sunshine. If a farmer plants the same seeds in rows, waters and nurtures them and makes sure weeds do not starve the crops, they will get a far better yield from the same amount of seeds and soil.

Once you have started to align the team in the direction you are heading as a business, you need to make sure they move towards the goal. There is nothing worse than a business putting lots of effort into something, then more or less abandoning it, thinking the course is set and it will get there on its own. Once you have planted the seed, nurture it so the crop will truly flourish.

Start with your management team. You need to be clear with them on what you want the company to stand for and, more importantly, why. They will then (hopefully) buy into this, but if any don't, you need to discuss it further and go through their reservations. It is much easier to steer a ship if there are six people helping.

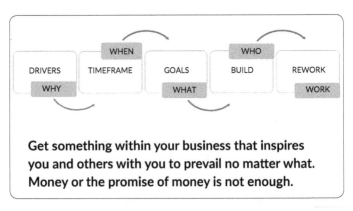

Get something within your business that inspires you and others with you to prevail no matter what. Money or the promise of money is not enough.

Then you and your managers want to look at getting the teams on board, as they will be the ones who really create the momentum. The chance to work on the 'big idea' is a powerful reason for people to be passionate and committed, and can be the glue that connects and binds them to the mission of the organisation. But first you need the managers to give their input, and own it.

I always suggest a managers' brainstorming session. They will probably come up with better goals or better ways of you achieving your goals than you can individually, which really gets them owning the goals. This alone is powerful (and remember they will be running and driving the business when you are on a Caribbean island, sipping a banana daiquiri).

You can't make people want something; all you can do is explain why you want it and hope they will follow. Make the business environment a place that people really get behind. There are lots of ways of making a business a better place, but start with the teams. You need to understand things from their point of view. You also need to understand what the customer really wants from a business. Ultimately, if the culture of the business is customer centric and the team gets behind this, then this will really help it flourish. All developments need to be met with the question, 'Is this customer centric enough?'

Once people start hearing that your business is a great place to work, they will naturally be attracted to it. This is a fundamental law of attraction.

SIDE NOTE – SHORT-TERM GAINS CAN CREATE LONG-TERM PROBLEMS

Make sure when you set your business environment up that you will walk the walk. If you offer people free drink and food, this must be for the long term. Taking it away will have a higher detrimental effect than if you don't do it at all.

If you don't really mean it, don't say you'll do it.

It can be difficult to come up with your core values – the things that will get the teams aligned behind you – so let the teams create them. Then they will own and buy into them. To do this effectively:

- Hire a conference or meeting room away from your premises. It must be outside your business premises so people can speak on a peer-to-peer level.

- Give people a rough outline of what you want to achieve, being careful not to introduce any bias. For example, you may want them to create five to eight core values they think the company should live and breathe. There are lots of tools, hand-outs etc that you can use in case people are struggling to find values. Email me at gc@gilescleverley.com and I will send you a list of 100 words that can help with a core values exercise.

- Give everyone a pack of Post-it notes (other brands are available), a pen and an A1 piece of paper.

- Ask everyone to write on the Post-it notes what they feel the company's core values are/should be and why.

- Once they have done this, get everyone to stick their poster up and explain each of their core values and the reason behind it. You may find many are similar.

- You can then mediate by getting a blank piece of A1 paper and moving people's Post-its onto yours, asking people which they think are most relevant.

- The result will be your core values.

The similarity between the values people will arrive at is mainly due to them buying into the business when they applied for the job. That's how they see and want the company to grow. This exercise is great for any type of planning and cultural shift, because everyone buys in as they are part of it, rather than just the executives coming up with 'another way of increasing profit'.

What do you then do with these values? I suggest you put them up where everyone can see them (this includes visitors). If you and your team really mean them, be proud of them. What is important is they are not just put on a poster and forgotten about.

Here are my top ten places for getting them out there:

- On your website
- Team meetings (using examples of how the values have been put into practice)
- Printed on cups and mugs
- Computer screensavers
- Have a different one explained each month in your newsletter
- Create treasure hunts and fun activities around them
- Intranet site
- Posters and plaques around the office or workspace
- In the recruitment process/adverts
- Front page of the employee handbook

Remember, if people are not living by your core values, they are probably not suited to the culture of the company. They can then be a thorn in the side of your company, and certainly of the department in which they work.

If you get this side right, it is amazing how people will be drawn to your organisation. Make your culture contagious not just for your staff, but for your clients and suppliers too.

Remember the key to success is not one big amazing idea that works, then away you go to untold riches. Rarely do people stumble upon the next Facebook or Google overnight. Success is lots of small decisions that culminate in the best version of your business. All these result in the business becoming the best version of you, so it can continue with or without you. I would encourage all businesses to have their own rules of the game to solidify the values. A really great book for this is *Winning* by Sir Clive Woodward.[11]

I am an advocate of setting dates and target goals, but when it comes to the culture of a business, this shouldn't be expressed in terms of 'by 20XX'. The culture of a company needs to be constantly nurtured, shaped and given the room to grow on its own. If you get the right people, you will be able to adapt for the future.

If I'd told you twenty years ago that a double figure percentage of people within a normal workforce would be on flexitime and have the chance to work remotely, you would likely have laughed me out of your office. We all need to make sure that as the world

---

11 C Woodward, *Winning: The path to Rugby World Cup glory* (Hodder & Stoughton, 2005)

flattens around us through technology, our businesses keep up. Being agile is key for any modern business.

Key takeaways

Goals are not for hiding in a drawer and forgetting about until next year. They need to be broadcast and evolved to keep everyone excited and build momentum within your company. And they must have buy-in and be owned by everyone.

In this chapter, we have looked at ways of building the all-important momentum and creating a culture that will naturally attract the right talent:

- Start with self-motivation before you can motivate your team.

- When you're clear on your why and have self-motivation behind it, pass that motivation on to your teams.

- Make sure your company culture supports your teams all pulling in the same direction.

- Your culture is also important when you're recruiting. You want it to attract A-grade employees and customers who are aligned with it.

- When you have recruited teams that align with your culture, lead by example and walk the talk.

- Use reviews to find out where employees feel they are, what they think of the company and where they see themselves in the future.

- Team-building events and rewards are great ways of growing morale and momentum. For most people, being acknowledged for their efforts is all they want.

- Once you have all your teams aligned with you, make sure your nurture the momentum so it continues to grow, even after you have left the business.

- Keep your teams motivated by keeping your word. If you don't mean it, don't say you'll do it.

- Involve you teams in creating the company values. That way, they will own them.

Now things are moving forward. Everyone understands the long-term goals of the business; you have momentum building and should be seeing improvements in the numbers (what gets measured improves). It's time to look into the final aspect: how to bring everything you have done so far together to catapult you to your ideal place, both personally and financially.

11
Time To Go!

Every area in someone's life (personal and business) can be restructured to make the most of their time, but I prefer to look beyond the basics of this. Firstly, you need to offload the things you do not like, which has the immediate effect of allowing you to enjoy your work and personal life more.

Look at what software or technology you can implement to save you time. Then look at what tasks you can delegate. But make sure that through offloading tasks, you do not neglect any of them. Delegating or outsourcing should always aim to improve the process.

The place to start when you're working towards freedom from your business is understanding where your time goes. Grab a blank piece of paper and write down all the things you do over the next two weeks. Ideally, use a template or a calendar to show the general flow of your day in blocks of time.

When you have your detailed view of where your time goes, you need to understand how the brain functions. You might think you are best when your back's against the wall and you're juggling lots of tasks in the air, but ultimately you will achieve more and be more efficient when you tackle tasks individually, giving them your focus. Once one task is complete, you can move on to the next. You need to get in flow for every task you do and get it nailed.

This is also how you need to make sure the people you are delegating to will work. There is nothing worse than someone having a desk with piles of paperwork everywhere. You need to make sure your teams' efficiency is at its best.

Once you've delegated the tasks that anyone can complete, you need to look at what tasks are left. Always think of time as a commodity. You want yours to be used as efficiently as possible on things you enjoy. After all, you are trying to work your way out of the business.

All your tasks need to be:

- Listed

- Process and procedure detailed

- Delegated

If you are looking at selling the business, many things that are higher level need to be detailed, but not necessarily delegated. As much as possible, you need to be working on the business, not in it.

Default diary

Focus on making sure the things you are responsible for are completed within the desired timeframe. It is so easy to get carried away with certain things, and then others get left until the last minute. I always recommend having a default diary. This is where you can schedule the monthly routines: what you need to get done in a day or week, the forthcoming meetings and the tasks that you like to do.

If you would like to do something, but never find the time to do it, you need to block this time out in your diary and make sure you stick to it. If you then let someone or something take the time away, you are the only one to blame. A default diary looks great on paper, but you must be disciplined to (a) stick to it and (b) not let others take from it.

				Week Commencing:_____	
WORKSH EET	MONDAY	TUESDAY	WEDNESDAY	THURSDAY	FRIDAY
			DAILY TASKS TO DO		
GOALS 20XX					
	MUST DO - Daily Tasks To Get Me To My Goals				

You can see from the example above that I have different sections for the day-to-day (default/weekly) tasks and areas to add and create each week (usually driven by longer-term goals).

A great trick is to print the default diary onto A4 or A5 sticky paper (depending on the size of your journal), then stick it in your journal every week. This makes sure the tasks are either completed or roll on to the next week. I am a fan of the digital diary, but sometimes you can't beat writing down the tasks at the beginning of the week to let your subconscious evaluate and mentally prepare for them.

Your default diary can be in Outlook (or any other digital calendar or app available) as recurring blocks every week. This way you make sure the routine tasks are always completed. If they're not, you can easily slip back into bad habits. Also, having your diary in an accessible digital format allows others to help schedule your time. You will know what hours of the day are your most productive, so I suggest you block the most important tasks in those hours.

Software

This can be the most obvious way of saving time, but for many people it is the most daunting. It can often take time to set up all the intricacies so auto-invoicing and quoting can be done, but you need to make the psychological breakthrough. Once you get over this hurdle, you will likely have an aha moment and wonder why you didn't do it years ago.

Many times over, I have heard clients say they are finding software difficult or it doesn't seem to work properly. Usually this is because it hasn't been set up properly, or the functions or workflows haven't been set up. I would recommend completing a full audit before looking at what other software to buy in.

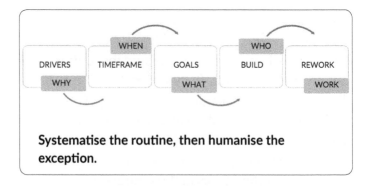

Generally, most software will give you a trial period, but this normally isn't long enough to let the software bed down and add value. There are two main things I would recommend before you make a decision:

Firstly, always take references. Ask the software provider for ten references of companies similar to yours that are using their product. This will give you a good gauge as to whether it is suitable for you.

Have a few questions prepared, but generally ask other business owners what their gut feeling is about the software. Ask how good the provider is at fixing issues. Most providers are great at offering you the world, but the proof is in the pudding of the repair/back-office team.

And secondly, prepare a list/brainstorm what you would like the software to do, whether it's to link to existing software, send auto-emails, plan people's day. Whatever it is, make a list. And remember to make the list for the future as you must be able to grow into the software. If you have fifty field engineers now, will it cater for 250? Will it help or hinder your growth?

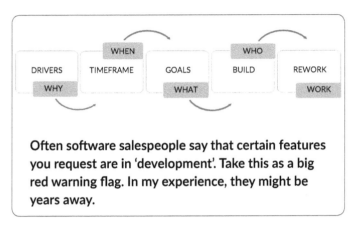

Often software salespeople say that certain features you request are in 'development'. Take this as a big red warning flag. In my experience, they might be years away.

Delegate

Delegation, not abdication. You need to get into the mindset of teaching others how to fish (showing them how to use a rod or a net), not just giving them the fish.

An example of this would be the basics of a stationery order. I don't know why, but often stationery ordering is the last job directors give to others. The best way to approach this is to write a manual on how you do it, making sure you include reminders and notes of how you complete the order (not just searches), how you feel about getting the best deals (not buying the cheapest as they don't last) etc. Whatever your preferences are. Remember, you can't get mad at people for not doing things that you haven't explained clearly or given written instructions to follow in a manual.

Two things you must remember:

- Manuals are there for a trainee to use in your absence to ensure consistency.

- Manuals can be altered, so if explanations in them do not flow, you can adjust them.

Do not fear people's reactions. They will like the support and clarity a detailed written manual gives them; their biggest fear is likely to be that they will look stupid by forgetting each step of what you have told them.

I could spend a whole book discussing time-saving processes. You can find over sixty-five time-saving tips at gilescleverley.com/resources. The main thing with saving time is always to strive for better. When you find yourself completing a repetitive task, investigate and see if it can be done better or differently by someone else or the correct software.

Key takeaways

Overall, you need to understand yourself and what you truly want deep down. Then get the team to understand and get them on board.

The thing with working your way out of your business is that there is no 100% foolproof method. Things will happen to scupper your plans. People will leave, sales might dip, hundreds of crises will come and go. At the time, they may feel like a complete nightmare. My advice is to keep your head up and push forward. I guarantee the harder something is to get through, the better you will feel on the other side.

Many people have lived before you. You are not the first person to have big dreams, so study others as much as you can, then build your actions on the back of the lessons you learn.

Everything in this book has proved true for me. If you follow the principles I've outlined, you're sure to move closer to the next stage of your business life: freedom. The only world that is real is your world. If you do not like the world you see, then change it. Don't blame anyone else or use excuses; go and change your world, and hopefully have a positive impact on others. Winners don't do different things, they do things differently.

Good luck, enjoy the ride and hold on tight!

Acknowledgements

To be able to grow we need to be uncomfortable, so I would like to thank all the people that have pushed me to grow, that have made me search and strive for betterment.

Thank you to the teams within my companies for their commitment and support, and allowing me the freedom to write and develop myself. I would like to thank the different coaches who have helped me through the years and kept me accountable.

Thanks to those who insisted I had to write this book, and my family for always believing in me.

Lastly I would like to thank the team at Rethink Press, for keeping me on track and having standards as high as mine.

The Author

Giles graduated with honours from Portsmouth University in 2002 and started his first 'proper' business within weeks. He has since founded and bought numerous businesses, and has also grown a property portfolio. Giles has dedicated over half of his life to learning about business, avidly reading, being coached and attending seminars for more than two decades. Throughout the years, he has unselfishly given his energy and resources to his colleagues, clients and partners.

Giles' philosophy on buying companies is to buy in business industries that he knows little about. There are three main reasons for this: firstly, you are forced to get the best people for the business, as you can't do the work yourself. Secondly, you can pull experience from other industries; and thirdly, and most importantly, you look at the business through virgin eyes. Virgin eyes are essentially the customer's eyes. This means that you don't have excuses or say, 'This is how we do things,' – you are purely looking from the customer's perspective and building the business for what they want. Boom: the brakes are released and the business flourishes!

Giles provides ongoing coaching and consulting to a number of prominent business executives and organisations. If you would like Giles to comment, write an article or be a guest on your show, you can reach him at:

✉ gc@gilescleverley.com

🌐 gilescleverley.com

Lightning Source UK Ltd.
Milton Keynes UK
UKHW022021051020
371060UK00010B/2613